D1170879

CADILLAC
and the
Founding of
DETROIT

1. *Cadillac*, a statue by Julius Melchers (1829-1908). (On the campus of Wayne State University)

CADILLAC
and the
Founding of
DETROIT

*Commemorating the Two Hundred and
Seventy-fifth Anniversary of the Founding
of the City of Detroit by Antoine Laumet
de Lamothe Cadillac on July 24, 1701*

*by Henry D. Brown, Henri Négrié, Frank R. Place,
René Toujas, Leonard N. Simons, Solan Weeks, and others*

*Published for the Detroit Historical Society
by Wayne State University Press, Detroit, 1976*

Library of Congress Cataloging in Publication Data
Main entry under title:

Cadillac and the founding of Detroit.

   1. Cadillac, Antoine de la Mothe, 1656 (ca.)–1730—
Addresses, essays, lectures. 2. Detroit—History—
Addresses, essays, lectures. I. Brown, Henry D.,
1910–   II. Detroit Historical Society.
F574.D453C332   977.4'34'010924 [B]   76-25500
ISBN 0-8143-1571-2

Contents

Illustrations

Foreword

In this Bicentennial year Americans have focused their attention on the founding of the United States, on the historic and dramatic episodes of the Revolution, and on the statesmen who created our republican form of government and provided the leadership which helped develop a national identity. In a similar manner, citizens of Detroit, one of the oldest settlements in middle America, have turned their interest to the founding and early development of their city. The establishment of Detroit in 1701 and the character of its founder, Antoine de Lamothe Cadillac, have captured the attention of students of Detroit history for more than a century. Two Frenchmen, René Toujas and Henri Négrié, have now added their studies to the earlier research of Lewis Cass, Silas Farmer, Clarence M. Burton, Levi Bishop, Milo Quaife, F. Clever Bald, George Paré, and Henry D. Brown. These two studies, completed during the past decade, shed light upon Cadillac's life in France prior to and after his return from North America. Toujas and Négrié also explain and justify Cadillac's successful efforts to obtain for himself the rank and prerogatives of the French nobility. The compilation of documentary material, as well as the articles by Toujas and Négrié, in this volume is a fitting memorial to the commemoration of Detroit's 275th anniversary. At the same time, it calls attention to the need for further study on the establishment of Detroit as a frontier outpost, its early history, and its founder.

Philip P. Mason
Wayne State University

MAIRIE DE SAINT NICOLAS-DE-LA-GRAVE
TARN-ET-GARONNE
Code Postal 8220

24 July 1976

Mr. Coleman A. Young, Mayor
City of Detroit   [post-dated]
U.S.A.

To the Honorable Mayor and Dear Colleague:

Today, the 24th of July, 1976, you are celebrating that famous day when Antoine Laumet, Chevalier de LaMothe Cadillac, approached your shores in order to found the city that you have the honor of administering.

I profit from this anniversary by remembering that since the year 1904 our two cities have been in regular communication. These completely amicable relations have prompted visitations back and forth.

The generosity of your compatriots has been evidenced at St. Nicolas-de-la-Grave in the mounting of a plaque on Cadillac's birthplace, the renovation of his birthplace, and most recently, the visit of your distinguished citizens at the inauguration of the Cadillac Museum.

The privileged bonds which unite our little village with your grand city originate then from this illustrious "Gascon" who, leaving the pleasant banks of the Garonne, crossed the ocean, went up the St. Lawrence to found, after numerous adventures, the settlement which over the course of the years has become your great city of Detroit.

Lastly, I congratulate you on this 275th anniversary which is celebrated with such spirit—it preserves in our souls the memory of our heroes and reaffirms again the friendship which unites our two cities.

I trust you will accept, Honorable Mayor and Dear Colleague, this expression of my highest esteem.

Jean LaFougere
Mayor of
St. Nicolas-de-la-Grave

Antoine de Lamothe Cadillac, as he chose to call himself, has suffered ennoblement from the pens of adulatory biographers and condemnation from those of censorious critics. He has been eulogized as a courageous French soldier who founded a great American city and as an arrogant self-seeker who accomplished nothing but deceit. The identical, very scattered bits of evidence have been used to document both points of view. Cadillac is known as the man who came with a handful of followers to build a city in the western wilderness where no settler had come before. He gathered disparate Indian tribes to promote trade, foreseeing the immense potential of the Great Lakes region, and devised a master plan to hold it for the benefit of his King and country. He took up the governorship of the colony of Louisiana and, through international commerce, attempted to make it into a thriving land. And he suffered imprisonment in the Bastille for speaking the truth against false investment schemes in the French colonies.

For whatever reasons, Cadillac made enemies among civil authorities and Jesuit missionaries whose letters and reports have given rise to speculations that he changed his name to cover a crime or personal difficulties, engaged in piracy off the Canadian coast, and stole other men's credentials. He has been accused of elaborating false credentials to get appointments, defrauding the Indians with brandy in exchange for beaver pelts that fattened his own purse, renouncing the basic principles of moral conduct, relentlessly opposing the Jesuit missionaries, and denouncing his enemies while flattering his patrons.

This volume is neither to refute nor to prove these charges, but rather to present a generous selection of the available materials that deal with significant aspects of the life and career of Cadillac. From these a balanced picture may emerge. The search for Cadillac has been enriched in recent years by the uncovering of hitherto unknown documents. A century ago Detroit's historian Levi Bishop reported on some of the first records that emerged from his inquiries.

Meeting of the Detroit Pioneer Society
Levi Bishop read the following interesting synopsis of his efforts to obtain information relative to Lamotte Cadillac, the founder of the City of Detroit:

Since our last meeting I have made efforts to procure additional information as to the founder of Detroit and his family. I sent copies of papers containing the proceedings of our last meeting and including a translation of the Cadillac deed and the letter of a daughter of Joseph Cadillac to the following persons: the mayor of Quebec; the Rev. Mr. Desnoyers, of St. Porte, Canada, from whom the Cadillac deed was received; to Minister Washburne, at Paris; the mayor of Castel Sarasin, in France; to the American Counsel at Marseilles; and the Mayor of Toulouse. To each of these persons I also wrote a letter calling their attention to the subject, and soliciting any information which they might possess, or might be able to obtain, in relation to the founder of Detroit, or his family . . . .

I still hope to get either an original portrait of Cadillac or a photograph from an original, which may be enlarged.

(Detroit Free Press, January 26, 1875)

Transcripts of archival materials held in France were forwarded to Levi Bishop by the American Counsul, and were later published by the Detroit historian Clarence M. Burton.

U. S. Consulate at Marseilles (France)

December 26, 1874

Levi Bishop, Esq.
President, Historical Society
Detroit

Dear Sir,

Immediately on the receipt of your favor of October 13 I wrote to the Mayor of Castel Sarasin, in the Department of Tarne and Garonne, transcribing *in extenso* your aforesaid letters. This morning only, I have received the Mayor's reply, copy of which is indorsed, conveying four documents referring to the family of Cadillac. These will no doubt prove interesting to you, and I hasten to transmit them without delay.

I regret being unable to furnish you a portrait of the late Antoine de Cadillac. I have caused researches to be made in museums and private collections, but as yet without result. Should, however, a copy of this portrait turn up I will not fail to buy it at once and forward it to you, of course, as a slight contribution and token of my admiration for the feeling which prompts you to make these researches in the interest of history, as well as, no doubt, with a view to reward merit even beyond the tomb . . . .

Be good enough to assure the honorable society over which you preside that I will leave nothing undone to promote their interests and that I shall do my best to gather information on this interesting subject and keep you duly informed of the result of my exertions.

Believe me faithfully yours,

(signed) *Frank W. Potter*
United States Consul

These researches have been continued by the citizens of Detroit who have served their city through the Historical Commission and the Detroit Historical Society. In the past few years there has been a quickening of interest. Working with the Commission, the Society has attempted to

2. Front page of *Le Messager*, March 14, 1875. The local newspaper of the district of Castelsarrasin, one hundred years ago, reported that new researches were under way on the life of Cadillac. One of the documents uncovered was Cadillac's death notice, reprinted in the newspaper, found in the registry of "Births, Marriages and Deaths" of Castelsarrasin's parish church of St. Sauveur. But, *Le Messager* still claims that Cadillac came from an old and noble family. (Original: Burton Historical Collection)

obtain once again as complete a record of documentation on Cadillac as possible. To this purpose, the Society and the Commission encouraged two French scholars of local history to investigate the documentary evidence for the life of Cadillac. Henri Négrié, past president of the Archaeological Society of the Department of Tarn-et-Garonne, undertook a biographical analysis which he reported to his Society and then gave to the Detroit Historical Society. From René Toujas, archivist of the Department of Haute-Garonne, the Detroit Society requested an archival study to establish the family and heritage of the Laumet-Cadillac families. An extension of this research resulted in a new review of Cadillac's career by Monsieur Toujas. The findings of these three reports are incorporated into the fabric of this volume.

Thus, the modest beginnings announced by the mayor of Castelsarrasin in 1874 have taken on a new dimension.

Mr. Frank W. Potter
United States Consul
Marseilles, France

Sir,

I have the honor to send you several extracts from the registers of the Mayoralty of Castel Sarasin in regard to the late Antoine de Lamotte Cadillac, who in 1701 founded the City of Detroit in the United States.

It has been impossible for me, notwithstanding all my researches, to find any more documents or any portrait of Lamotte Cadillac, not knowing of any of his descendants in this part of the country. Be so good, Honorable Consul, as to excuse my delay in answering your letter of the 28th of October last. It has been occasioned only by the wish to make the fullest possible response to the recollections which the City of Detroit still maintains and cherishes for one of the inhabitants of the city of Castel Sarasin.

Unfortunately I can find nothing more, and I beg to assure you that the city of Castel Sarasin is deeply sensible of the honor of seeing the memory of one of her sons thus maintained by the city of Detroit.

Please accept, Mr. Consul, my very distinguished sentiments.

The Mayor
(signed) *A. Boé, Adjutant*

A chronicle of the career of Cadillac is provided, giving the basic annals of his life with an accompanying commentary composed of excerpts from documents, reports, letters, memoranda, modern interpretations, and recent descriptions to flesh out the bare bones of chronology. Richard Place of Wayne State University, Department of History, contributes an historical essay. Separate sections are devoted to Cadillac's descendants, a description of Cadillac's homeland at the beginning of this century by the then president of the Historical Society, and a summary of the archaeological report on the excavations in search of Cadillac's tomb in the Carmelite building at Castelsarrasin. Solan Weeks, Director of the Detroit Historical Museum, has written the fascinating story of the purchase, renovation, and dedication of the house in St. Nicolas-de-la-Grave by the citizens of Detroit. Present at the commemorative ceremonies, Weeks was an active participant in establishing this tangible link between Detroit and the city that witnessed the birth of Detroit's founder. A dictionary of names precedes the chronicle. A glossary of special terms, a listing of archival sources, and abbreviations are appended to assist the reader.

Biography is an art rather than a science. Hence, not only may

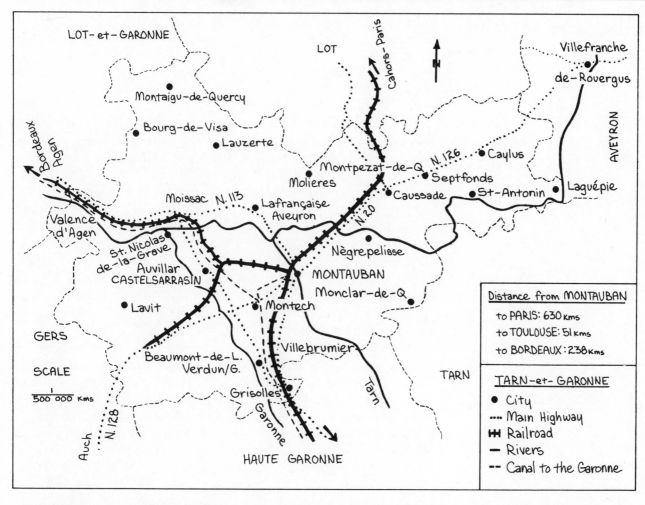

3. Map indicating region of
St. Nicolas-de-la-Grave.

assessments of a man differ, but they may also stand in rigorous opposition to each other. A portion of the bitter conclusions of the late Jesuit Father Delanglez of Loyola University is provided along with a more balanced, non-polemical characterization by Leonard N. Simons, president of the Detroit Historical Commission. In the final analysis the reader must decide to what extent Cadillac was less than a saint and more than a scoundrel.

No compilation of a variety of material can be completed without the generous assistance of many hands. Richard Place, Muriel N. Robinove, Samuel Scott, and William Bostick are the careful translators of many of the documents and essays. William Bostick, of the Detroit Institute of Arts, also contributed the sketches he made at the sites in France. Leonard N. Simons provided full access to his extensive files and personal library, as well as to his time and knowledge of the history of Detroit. Mrs. Alice Dalligan of the Burton Historical Collection, Detroit Public Library, allowed full use of the extensive holdings in her charge.

To all of the above contributors, to the citizens of Detroit, and to the citizens of St. Nicolas-de-la-Grave, this volume is presented in commemoration of the two hundred and seventy-fifth anniversary of the founding of the City of the Straits by Antoine Laumet de Lamothe Cadillac on July 24, 1701.

July 24, 1976   *13*

Cadillac's Homeland

Henry D. Brown

In June, 1961, Henry D. Brown, then director of the Detroit Historical Commission, filmed the sites and countryside that were the setting for Cadillac's first and last years. His report, from which the following is excerpted, appeared in the Bulletin *of the Detroit Historical Society, XVIII, March, 1962.*

For over a half-century, individuals interested in Detroit history have journeyed to Cadillac's homeland, in South Central France, to obtain information on our town founder. The first official journey was made in 1907, by City Historiographer Clarence M. Burton. His account was published in the 1911 *Michigan Pioneer and Historical Collections;* John Hubert Greusel visited in 1924 and prepared a pamphlet account "Mystery of Cadillac's Lost Grave." The 1955 visit of Milo Quaife and the 1958 visit of Reuben Ryding are recorded in the *Bulletin* of the Detroit Historical Society [Vol. XI, No. 4 and Vol. XIII, No. 1].

When Cadillac returned to France, he left Louisiana by the ship *Paon* in late May 1717, and reached the French port of LaRochelle on September 1, 1717, an elapsed time of some three months. In contrast, my trip by Air France took just over nine hours of flying time from Detroit.

Our first full day, June 15, was a very full day—beginning with a pleasant official visit with Mayor Adrien Alary of Castelsarrasin, who had been our guest here in Detroit three year previous. M. Eugene Redon had been designated by the mayor to assist us in our project, and from this time forward, he accompanied us on most of our excursions. M. Redon is an amateur archaeologist and member of the Société Archéologique de Tarn-et-Garonne. He is primarily concerned with pre-history archaeology, but had recently supervised excavation of a grave in the one-time Carmelite Monastery, where Cadillac is known to have been buried. We examined this site with him. Since the French Revolution, the Monastery has been converted to secular use, for many years it served as a prison, and is now used for various city functions. This past spring, excavation for building alterations revealed burials, and M. Redon was called in to supervise the excavations and prepare a report. They found two levels of burials; at the lower level was a single burial, with nails of a casket, and a portion of a skull. Study of the skull indicated that it was of a man between 70-80. They have conjectured that this might be the remains of Cadillac because the single burial reflects the importance of the subject, and the age of the subject as indicated by study of the skull. (Cadillac was 72 at time of death.) As many important people were buried in the Monastery in the early days, this can only be conjecture, with the limited evidence now at hand.

Just outside the village of Caumont is a group of three farms, and related farm buildings, still designated on government topographical survey maps as "Laumets." This emphasizes the mystery of Cadillac's name. As far as is known, he never used the name Cadillac until after coming to the new world. After his thirty years in America, the name Cadillac was evidently accepted upon his return to his homeland, where he lived for another thirteen years, and enjoyed considerable prominence.

Cadillac's homeland was at the boundary line of three ancient

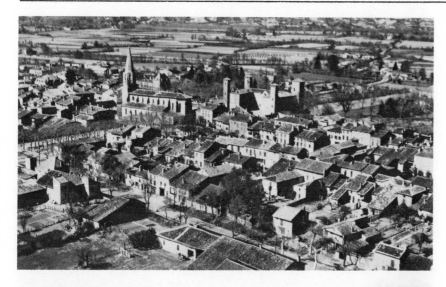

Henry D. Brown

4. View of St. Nicolas-de-la-Grave.

5. The late 17th-century church spire rises above the streets of St. Nicolas-de-la-Grave.

French provinces. To the west, toward the Atlantic, is the province of Gascony, and Cadillac is often referred to as having a Gascon temperament. To the east and south on the Garonne River is the province of Languedoc. Some thirty miles southeast is the capital of Toulouse. North is the province of Quercy. On maps of the 1600s and early 1700s, the village of St. Nicolas sometimes is included in one or the other of these provinces. The customs here are a combination of the customs of the several provinces.

The architecture shows influence of Languedoc with octagonal church spires or towers, and buildings built of a soft red brick. Other church buildings show the Gascon influence, with strong suggestion of the Spanish. Here church facades rise above the building, and are pierced with openings for bells. Buildings are often stuccoed with white. The principal churches of both St. Nicolas and Castelsarrasin have the octagonal tower.   *15*

6. Rue Lamothe Cadillac,
St. Nicolas-de-la-Grave, France.
The small house on the left side with the
plaque above the door is Cadillac's
birthplace. Watercolor by
William A. Bostick.

The church at St. Nicolas has been stuccoed while that of Castelsarrasin is red brick. A chapel just outside St. Nicolas has the high facade pierced with niches for bells, as do churches at nearby Castelmayran at St. Aignan.

Visits to St. Nicolas on several succeeding days provided a variety of experiences. The beautiful church where Cadillac was baptized, with its octagon bell tower spire, of the style common throughout the ancient province of Languedoc, had much of its interior "modernized" a century ago, but it still retains elements of the simple dignity of the period of its construction 600 years ago. We filmed the house with the plaque stating Cadillac was born there, and found that, as was the case six years previously, the building was still used as a junk shop. Evidence indicates that the building was once two stories high, but many years ago was reduced to one story. Only the old kitchen fireplace appears to date from Cadillac's time. The problem of proving that this building was actually Cadillac's birthplace is still unsolved. The baptism record is in the office of the Mayor. There is also a town plat book made more than 60 years after Cadillac's death which indicates this house was owned by his mother's family. Oral tradition of a small village, which has remained little changed for 300 years, was the basis for the statement on the plaque designating this house.

We visited the ancient and historic city of Montauban twenty miles East of St. Nicolas. Here is located the "College des Jesuites" which the Canon believes was the school Cadillac attended. The Tarn River, which divides from the Garonne just above St. Nicolas is spanned at Montauban by a brick bridge (pont Vieux) which was old in Cadillac's time. He would probably have used the river to travel there.

A most unusual occurrence was a visit to the home of Counte Armand de Pouzarques, a great-great-great grandson of Cadillac, who was 90 years old. In his younger years, he had spent a number of years in the United States and spoke excellent English, with delightfully unexpected colloquial expressions. Although keenly conscious now of his Cadillac heritage, he had then been so uninterested that he had never visited Detroit.

Mayor Jean La Fougere of St. Nicolas-de-la-Grave conducted us on a tour north over the Garonne River, to the high bluff overlooking the valley, the site of an old Roman Road. Here we could see the confluence of the Tarn and the Garonne rivers to the west. Southwest the white stucco and light stone buildings of Castelsarrasin gleamed in the distance. Directly south, some three miles, on the first rise of ground was the little village of St. Nicolas.

The Extraordinary Career of the Gascon Lamothe-Cadillac, Founder of Detroit

René Toujas

This translation has been abridged with the kind permission of René Toujas from his booklet Le Destin extraordinaire du gascon Lamothe-Cadillac, fondateur de Detroit, *Montauban, 1974.*

When the city of Detroit celebrated its bicentennial in 1901, the Archaeological Society of Tarn-et-Garonne gathered much new information about Cadillac from the local archives. The Society discovered that he had lived in America under an assumed name: his brilliant genealogy was an invention. Cadillac entered this world prosaically as Antoine Laumet, the son of a small town judge in the pleasant community of St. Nicolas-de-la-Grave, in the shadows of the towers of the handsome chateau named for Richard the Lion-Hearted. Guided by a cadastral map of the second half of the 18th-century, the Society located the house where he was born in a little street bordering upon the public square.

In further celebration of Detroit's 1901 bicentennial, the Archaeological Society, presided over by the Canon Pottier, organized a ceremony in the course of which the street was renamed Lamothe-Cadillac and a commemorative plaque was mounted on the Laumet house. It was the first public homage rendered by the Gascons of Tarn-et-Garonne to one of their most illustrious, but hitherto unrecognized, sons. Later, the town of Castelsarrasin also honored Cadillac when it bestowed his name upon the square in front of the solid, comfortable house in which he lived out the last years of a long and adventurous life.

Antoine Laumet was born at St. Nicolas-de-la-Grave on March 5, 1658. His father, Jean Laumet, came from a family of merchants and was born in Lomagne at Caumont, a neighboring community of St. Nicolas. He was a lawyer in the Toulouse parliament when he married Jeanne Péchagut on August 19, 1646. She was the daughter of a landowner of St. Nicolas and of Ann Gibrac, sister of the town clerk of Castelsarrasin. Jean Laumet began his career as a manorial judge in his native village in 1650. In 1652, after a brief stay in Castelsarrasin, he obtained the office of assistant to the judge for the St. Nicolas area from its lord, the abbot of Moissac. The protection of the abbey's administrator—who was Cardinal Mazarin, chief minister to the young Louis XIV—could only help his career. In 1653, in the midst of the Fronde, when the opposing armies were ravaging the Garonne valley leaving misery and epidemic in their wake, Jean Laumet was appointed first consul of the community. During these particularly difficult times, the selection was a testimony of great confidence. Finally, in 1664, he was appointed judge of St. Nicolas. In addition to his obligation as magistrate and public figure, Jean Laumet enjoyed fully the life of a country gentleman, but he soon found himself saddled with debts—explained no doubt by family obligations, for he had at least eight children.

Unfortunately, no documents from the youth of Cadillac were found. The spirited, often biting, style of the letters he wrote with such ease during his stay in the New World, the culture—sacred as well as profane—that he demonstrated, all lead to the conclusion that he had a good secondary education. Possibly, he was a student at the Doctrinal College at Moissac or, more likely, at l'Esquile in Toulouse where one of the professors was a friend of his father.

Little is known about the arrival of Cadillac in America and about his early years in France. He claimed to have landed in 1683 at Port Royal, capital of Acadia, a peninsula in eastern Canada that served as a base of privateering against the shipping of the English colonists. It is possible therefore that he was a member of a privateering crew, as well as having led the adventurous life of a *coureur de bois*, travelling through the English colonies as indicated in his detailed reports on Boston and New York. His description of Boston is a worthy example:

> two-thirds of the city is built of wood and the rest in brick or stone; the houses are pleasant and very neat; it is inhabited by merchants and sailors. There are very few gentlemen. The mainstay of their commerce is the fish taken for the most part along the coasts of Acadia. They have many slaves, negroes and negresses, who were brought here in the early days of the colony and have multiplied.

Cadillac concluded his study of Boston's population with the prophetic judgment that "They are republican in their souls and are the sworn enemies of tyranny." While in New York, "a city built in brick, almost all of

7. The citizens of
St. Nicolas-de-la-Grave, 1901.
The community posed for its portrait in the court of the city hall in celebration of the bicentenary of the founding of Detroit by Cadillac.

8. The Jesuit School in Montauban. Cadillac may have received his early schooling here. Watercolor by Gibien. (Original: Burton Historical Collection)

whose inhabitants are Dutch," he lived among the French Protestant refugees engaged in trade.

Lacking all records, we cannot explain why the well-informed governor of the territory, Louis Alexandre de Friches, Chevalier de Ménneval wrote that "this Cadillac, the most malicious person in the world, is a wild man driven from France for who knows what crimes."

Established in Port Royal, he sold brandy to and traded with the Canibas Indians on the Acadian frontier, which he commanded during the Anglo-French War. Later he boasted that he "would have assuredly given the English some anxious moments and . . . have gone as far as Boston." He was also involved with Canadian privateers, particularly with Denis Guyon. His marriage contract of June 25, 1687, is the first public document of his stay in New France, and here is met for the first time under his new name. In 1688 he returned to Acadia with a grant of land in the vicinity of Port Royal called "les Douagues which he renamed La Mothe." Two years later an English army laid it waste.

After his marriage, Cadillac attempted to enter the legal profession, to the loud complaints of Governor de Ménneval. Des Gouttins, the newly appointed judge of Port Royal, "took it into his head," wrote the governor on September 7, 1689, to the Minister of Marine,

to appoint M. Cadillac as notary and court clerk contrary to my advice and prohibition. And, because I have told him [Des Gouttins] that he [Cadillac] was a rascal and a mendacious spirit entirely capable of embroiling these poor people in a thousand chicaneries and suits in order to profit therefrom, and that I would not allow it, he [Cadillac] has gone to Quebec on another pretext to obtain, so I have been told, letters enabling him to exercise these charges despite me.

Renewed hostilities between France and England profoundly affected Cadillac's plans. Sent on a tactical voyage off the coast of Acadia, Cadillac's ship was forced out to sea and eventually landed him in France. "I am here without money," he wrote from his involuntary exile in Rochefort, finding my subsistence only on credit that will not last long. For this voyage whose purpose was unknown to me, I have left my wife, my family, and my estate without providing for their necessities in the expectation that I would return to Port Royal in a month.

In Paris he assumed the rank of captain of the infantry. Perhaps he appropriated the service record of his older brother. De Ménneval's complaints against him had also reached Paris, but Cadillac must have argued his case well, as a note written by a clerk at the beginning of 1690 indicates.

This Cadillac is at present in the entourage of Monseigneur, having found himself in France unexpectedly because of the unforeseen visit of M. de La Caffinière's ship. He was on board because he almost alone knows the coasts of New York and New England and was judged absolutely indispensable for the mission which they intended to carry out when they left Port Royal. He is an adventurer who has explored northern America and done so with application and brought back reasonably exact information.

We think it would be both charitable and just for Monseigneur to give him something for his trip; he has existed on loans during the six months that he has been in France; he has about used them up and is in real need. It should also be pointed out that if at some later time we wish to undertake some action against New York or New England, he will be a necessary actor because of his detailed knowledge of the coasts and ports.

Finally, the chance was offered for an honorable career in America. "There is reason to hope," concluded the writer of the note, "that having been warned that he cannot avoid punishment should he return to his old ways, he will become a good citizen who can be of service in case Port Royal is attacked."

Thus, his involuntary visit to France at the end of 1689 represents an extremely important event in Cadillac's life, for it enabled him to form useful relations with certain officials of the Ministry of Marine—among others Lagny and Latouche—who were taken with his exceptional intelligence and imagination. Thanks to their protection he became an officer of the Marines in Canada.

Trusting in the Minister's protection, Cadillac rejoined his family in Port Royal, and then departed Acadia for good in July, 1691. Upon his arrival in Canada, he was immediately named to fill a vacant lieutenancy while he awaited the arrival of the king's commissions. To justify his integration into the Canadian Army, the authorities of New France recognized "the great services he had rendered in Acadia" and the fact—more controversial—that he had been a lieutenant in France. Thus, the Court's instructions to Governor Frontenac were applied with alacrity.

His Majesty, having been informed that during the absence of M. de Lamothe Cadillac, gentleman of Acadia, his lands have been ruined, will be pleased if sieur Frontenac gives him employment in whatever he judges appropriate for his service and that he assist him in any way he can.

Dressed once more in the prestigious uniform of an officer, Cadillac passed only the winter of 1691 in Quebec. Actually he participated actively in the elaboration of a plan to attack the English colony at New York—a plan that Callière, commandant of Montreal, had fancied since January 1689. Called back to Paris in April of 1692, Cadillac conferred with the officials in the Ministry of Marine. Cadillac was to advise on two armed ships that were to spy out the American coast. Frontenac, in a letter dated September 15, 1692, gave some precise details on the progress of this campaign to study the coastal waters.

So that Villebon more certainly executes his instructions to cruise the coasts of Boston and Manhattan, I ordered him to join with the sieur d'Iberville so that they can more readily handle any ships they meet and be ready to do whatever they judge necessary. As you have instructed me, I will have the sieur de Lamothe taken on board along with the mapmaker [Jean-Baptiste Franquelin] who has made all the maps and charts of Manhattan and Orange so that they can be corrected while cruising the coasts.

On November 16, 1692, d'Iberville cruised off Boston. One month later to the day, he dropped anchor off Saint-Martin-de-Ré with Cadillac on board. Cadillac presented the Ministry with maps of Boston and Manhattan, as well as a chart of the American coastline from Acadia to Virginia. He also submitted a memorandum on Acadia and New England in which he argued that the capture of Boston was less crucial than that of Manhattan which would not only bring about the ruin of the Iroquois but of all New England. The effect of his presentation is apparent in a memorandum from the king to the governor of New France.

The sieur de Lamothe Cadillac has rendered an account of all that pertains to the condition of New England and New York. He has furnished memoirs which will be useful at the proper time and place. He has also described the state of the bays, roads, rivers, ports, and harbors of these regions, and of Acadia. It remains to make accurate charts of the Gulf of St. Lawrence and the surrounding shoreline to the north and south from the river entrance to Quebec. We must carefully gather all the information that practical men have so that Cadillac can prepare charts and verify those made from memory in order to rectify them where necessary. Send copies of everything.

The benefits for his career of Cadillac's second visit to Paris were quickly forthcoming when the new Minister of Marine, Pontchartrain, promised him the first vacant company in Canada, and no doubt was instrumental in his promotion in grade upon his return to Quebec at the end of July, 1693. Frontenac gave command of Michilimackinac to this man whom he described as being "of distinction, of great capacity and worth," and with the necessary characteristics of "adroitness, firmness and tact." Taking up his new post, Cadillac quickly set out to familiarize himself with the land. "Mapping all the regions, lakes and rivers, recording observations that I am sure until now have not been known," as he described it to Joseph Latouche of the Ministry of Marine. In another letter addressed to Roland de Lagny, he stated his intention that

> when I have traversed this country, I will be better able to speak of what I have seen. Regarding the lakes, rivers, different tribes, maxims, customs, interests, inclinations, and other things noteworthy, you will see a chart with so clear an explanation that henceforth you will speak as shrewdly about it as if you had been to these places.

In the course of his exploration of the up-country, Cadillac developed the idea that the occupation of the Great Lakes region and the establishment of a French commercial center to rival New York would thwart the English influence among the Indian tribes of the West. Therefore, he pressed for permission to cross the Atlantic and present his views at Court. At this time the market for beaver was saturated. The French took measures to reduce the flow of up-country furs into the colony by suppressing all trading permits and closing almost all the western posts, including Michilimackinac. At the end of August, 1697, Cadillac therefore returned to Montreal with a troop of three hundred Indians intended to reinforce Quebec's defenses against a possible English attack. In the following year Cadillac, on his own request, sailed for France. By this time he had clearly decided to carry out the plan that was to make him famous: the founding of Detroit on the river connecting the Lakes Huron and Erie. It is certain that the idea had come to him during his stay at Michilimackinac. He had explored the extent of his command and beyond to the limits of the Great Lakes. Favored as the region was with a temperate climate, he had seen its economic and strategic importance. The official résumé of the first written document treating his project for the founding of Detroit, that he presented in Paris in December, 1698, reads as follows.

> He offers to gather all our savage allies who are presently scattered to the north of Lake Huron and in the vicinity of Lake Superior into their former territory situated between Lake Erie, Lake Huron, and the Lake of the Illinois[Michigan] and to create at Detroit a fortified post as the chief place of the colony.

The suggested regrouping of the Indians on their former hunting grounds was clever because it would permit the French to extend their influence in the important commercial crossroads of the Great Lakes region. Cadillac also stressed the military advantage stemming from the presence of a French garrison and a good number of Indian friends in this

23

region with its mild climate. They would reduce the threat from the Iroquois who had always harassed the colony and prevented its aggrandizement. The plan would also encourage the Indian allies to hunt in the enemy's zone of influence, some hundreds of kilometers to the south of Lake Erie. Finally, the waters of all the lakes pass through the Detroit River which was the only practical route whereby the English could trade with the tribes under French protection. According to Cadillac, control of these narrows would be the best way to stifle English commerce by depriving them of a major source of pelts.

Cadillac also insisted on the economic advantage of his plan for a French market now saturated with beaver skins "as much because of the too great quantity as of the poor quality." His rationale was very simple: the regrouping of the Indians occupied in making their camps and reestablishing their lands would effect a reduction, if not the cessation, of the beaver trade for two or three years. This argument could not fail to appeal to the minister embarrassed by the glut of furs in France. Cadillac's memoir abounded in technical details, as if he wished to give some lessons in the breeding of beaver to those having an interest in the Company of the Colony. He took up again the claim of the Canadian colonists for the reestablishment of the twenty-five trading licenses, "that is to say, permit twenty-five canoes of three men each to carry merchandise to the post that will be established. It is evident," he went on, "that all the savages being massed in one place, the traders would not think to go further because they will have found all that they look for, which is the beaver." It would therefore be a means of reducing the number of *coureurs de bois*.

Finally, Cadillac proposed that they instruct the Indians in the French language and make them as French as the other subjects of the king. He foresaw the application of the principle of *cujus regio ejus religio* (who owns the land, supplies the religion); they would become Christians. It would then be possible to encourage the marriage of Frenchmen with Indian women as the best way to consolidate power.

Receiving the Court's approval, subject to consideration by the officials in Quebec, Cadillac sailed for Canada in the spring of 1699. Governor Callière, although pronouncing his approval, viewed the project as premature, while the concerned citizens vigorously opposed it. Cadillac returned to Versailles at the end of 1699 only to be rebuked by Pontchartrain. Whereupon Cadillac enlarged upon his arguments for founding the post, supported by Pontchartrain who was advised that the English wished to seize the straits. Pontchartrain informed Cadillac,

The King has reexamined your project and has ordered me to send you immediately to Canada to take prompt possession of the straits, intending that you command there until further orders; as quickly as possible you are to embark at Rochefort.

Although displeased with the order for Cadillac to found a colony at the straits, Callière confirmed the departure of the expedition in the coming spring. He made an unsuccessful effort to have de Tonti replace Cadillac.

René Toujas

9. *The Landing of Cadillac.* This watercolor by Léo Boistel for a dedicatory poem written by M. Sémézies formed part of a presentation volume given by the Archaeological Society of Tarn-et-Garonne, bearing the title "Hommage de la société archéologique à la ville de Détroit." The volume was received by Mayor William Maybury in 1905, and is now in the Burton Historical Collection.

Fully in command, Cadillac quit the capital of New France on May 8, 1701, arriving on July 24 at the future site of Detroit. After wintering there, he returned to Quebec the following summer. Cadillac reported that fall wheat and spring wheat, "as is grown in Canada," and Indian corn provided the basis for the colony's independent food supply. "The land being sworn and having announced that it is necessary to follow the growing practices of France," wrote Cadillac, "I have left orders to commence the planting [of wheat] around the 20th of September." When the governor learned of the meager results of the first harvest of wheat and Indian corn, however, he was much less optimistic than was Cadillac. He ordered in July 1702 that only twenty-five soldiers and a sergeant be left in Detroit.

While encouraging the resettlement of the allied Indian tribes around Detroit (a program supported by Governor Callière when he met with the Indian chiefs at Montreal), Cadillac clearly desired a permanent French population, and he resorted to one of his masterful graphic illustrations to present his case:

> If this post is established with Frenchmen and Indians, it will secure our trade with the allies and provide the club that will overpower the Iroquois. It is impossible that our families can remain in a place inhabited only by Indians; their misery would be extreme and without relief.

Thus, in the spring of 1703 he revived his project for the settlement of six families. The directors of the Company of the Colony had promised to give these settlers trade goods at a price one-third lower than that offered the Indians. In return they were obligated to sell whatever beaver and other pelts their trade provided to the Company's clerk.

Cadillac, for his part, was directing his efforts toward obtaining a trade monopoly in the Great Lakes region while substituting himself for the Company of the Colony. The Company was not allowed to trade outside the fort at Detroit so as not to ruin Montreal's trade. He tried to convince the minister that Canada had always known that

> the Detroit post is incontestably the most suitable for security of trade and for the fertility of its soil; if it is left alone with a sufficient force there is nothing to fear either from our allies or from the enemies of the State. It seems to me that your intention in establishing Detroit was to reassemble there the tribes and particularly the Michilimackinac post.

Thus, he openly affirmed his desire to profit from the royal policy to reduce the beaver trade by requesting the suppression of all other western trading posts, including his former command which remained the religious capital of the up-country.

Immediately he encountered fierce resistance from the Jesuits who opposed the resettlement of the native tribes at Detroit. The governor, in the course of the summer of 1702, summoned Cadillac, Father Vaillant—the Jesuit superior—and the two directors of the Company to a conference to seek a solution. The representatives of the Company indicated that if the Michilimackinac mission were transferred to Detroit, they would assume the cost. They hoped to acquire the greatest part of that trade "which will serve to compensate for the expenses that they would incur." Less naive, the intendant Champigny declared that the king had given orders for the establishment of Detroit without wishing the destruction of Michilimackinac and the other posts. Cadillac contested this vigorously and made the reunion of the allied tribes at Detroit the condition for success of his new settlement.

Callière disposed of the question with a compromise which gave Cadillac the title of commander general of Detroit and of all the other posts of the up-country. Until the end of French domination, Detroit was the civil and military capital of the western territories.

Predictably, the compromise with the Jesuits was scarcely implemented. Cadillac claimed that the Jesuits refused to come to Detroit; the Jesuits proclaimed that Cadillac had come to Detroit only to sell his merchandise, after which he would return to Montreal. Certainly the temptation was great to trade with the tribes in the English zone of influence, perhaps even in contraband—as Governor Vaudreuil, Callière's successor, accused Cadillac of doing. The accusation is a reasonable explanation for the diminution of the beaver harvest. The Company suspected that Cadillac had found ways to ship as many furs as he wished under assumed names and even by using Indians. The complaints against Cadillac were all the more believable because such activity was easily accomplished from Detroit. As its founder had said, "it is the only place from which to go among all the tribes of the lake region and it is the entrance and exit for trade with all our allies."

In his audience of 1703 with Pontchartrain, Cadillac did not hesitate to argue forcefully that it was necessary to create a solid post sustained by a sizeable garrison, left free to establish itself without the burden of the trading licenses and without suffering from another establishment in the up-country. Unfortunately, these ideas were in complete contradiction with the policy followed by the governors. They desired only a return to the traditional system of trading licenses and advanced military posts, including Detroit. Finally, Cadillac proposed, solely in the interest of the Company he maintained, to substitute himself in its place and promised compensation. He promised to pay the Company in cash from his advances provided that it would honor the letters of exchange from the beaver trade that he would remit to it every year.

Pontchartrain solicited the advice in this matter of the former intendant Champigny who was now in France as his advisor. While Pontchartrain openly stated that he was of a mind to support the operation and leave entire responsibility for it to Cadillac, Champigny argued that it would be unfair to the Company that had made a large investment in the creation of the post, and that the commandant wanted the Company out only because he wanted to fill his own pockets. "I have no doubt," he observed with undeniable perception, "that if Sr. de Lamothe had thought that this post would be united to the colony, he would not have gone there because that arrangement would not accommodate his intentions."

Before making a decision that would determine Cadillac's future, the Minister also sought the opinion of the financier Bouvier. The latter portrayed the situation truthfully: "no one can deny that the post at Detroit is located in the midst of the Indian tribes. The colony will never be freed from its just fear that the proprietor of the new territory is the absolute master of the beaver trade." However, it seemed to him natural and even indispensable to leave this trade depot in the hands of Cadillac. With this background, Ponchartrain notified Cadillac he was to have full command of the post.

Cadillac, enjoying the firm and constant support of the Minister, vigorously defended himself to the governor who was constrained to lecture Father Marest for not respecting the accord of 1702: "The Court desires the Detroit establishment; that can give me only pleasure. I exhort you to get along with M. de Lamothe as well as you possibly can." He reminded Father Marest that the commander of Detroit was the sole judge of the advisability of the Ottawa coming to Cadillac's post and invited him to follow the Indians when they located there.

27

When war broke out in the West, the Ottawas attacked the fort at Detroit and killed three Frenchmen. The court requested Vaudreuil to act in concert with Cadillac on the measures necessary to restore good relations between the French and the Indians "because that served the interests of the colony." In their report of 1707, the governor and the superintendent eagerly seized the opportunity to undermine Cadillac through the Minister.

> M. de Lamothe is hated by the troops, the settlers, and the savages who regard him as an avaricious man, to put it mildly. He grants licenses to those he sends with canoes to trade in the remote regions of the lakes when that trade is prohibited to him. The authorities do not know what becomes of the beaver that he takes at Detroit as well as elsewhere because this post supplies a very small quantity to the central office. This year he has supplied only six hundred pounds worth.

On the other hand, the Court was already disturbed about the alcohol trade with the Indians of Detroit, and "His Majesty expects absolute adherence to his prohibition against carrying brandy to the Indians." Violations of royal regulations led the minister to send commissioner Clairambault d'Aigremont to Detroit in November, 1707, to investigate the situation. From this point on, Pontchartrain became increasingly suspicious of his *protégé*, while continuing to emphasize the importance of the French presence in the Great Lakes region.

Fearing the consequences of Clairambault's inspection, Cadillac took the path of recognizing his own guilt. "It is said," he frankly wrote to the Minister, speaking of himself in the third person, "that he has made large profits while in Detroit; while that may be, one ought not bother to repeat it, seeing the troubles and the cares that he has borne." He criticised Clairambault at length for not having tried to understand, through long discussions, the reasons that made him act as he did. He insisted often that the companies of Indians be constituted "on the same footing as those of the French" and led by "the Indians who have the most prestige in the tribe." He also suggested in 1708 that five or six hundred settlers and a proportionate number of troops were needed to fortify both sides of the passage through the straits. Finally, he hoped to encourage the marriage between the French and "instructed" Indian maidens.

In November, 1708, Clairambault drew up his indictment: he treated Cadillac as an adventurer whose policy endangered the entire French domination in the territories of the interior and accused him of having turned Detroit into an economic satellite of New York. This memorandum was an express condemnation of the expansionist policy adopted by the government after the peace of 1700. Thus it was difficult for Pontchartrain openly to disavow the architect of this quest for an imperial frontier. The King's memoir of July 6, 1709, revealed the royal embarrassment. First he noted with satisfaction the advanced stage of Detroit, which should serve as a model for others. Homage to Cadillac rendered, he then ordered troops stationed at Detroit to return to Montreal, as a gesture to the

Canadian authorities. Moreover, a particularly sharp letter from Raudot convinced the minister of the impossibility of keeping Cadillac in Detroit any longer.

Realizing the need to assign Cadillac a post outside Canada, the King appointed him to the newly vacated governorship of Louisiana. Cadillac was ordered on November 3, 1710, to proceed immediately to Louisiana, but he delayed for a full year before leaving for France. He was never again to set foot on Canadian soil. Cadillac quickly appreciated the immense advantages offered his career by interesting the financier Antoine Crozat in the future of Louisiana. Convinced, Crozat acquired a trade monopoly in the colony for fifteen years.

At the beginning of 1713 Cadillac sailed for Louisiana, where he found an almost unknown land, its riches scarcely catalogued. Vigorous as ever, he displayed his usual dynamism, but he also found himself at odds with the important officials of the colony, as well as with the Indians of the region. Conflict with Crozat was also inevitable, for while Cadillac wanted to trade with his Spanish neighbors, Crozat insisted on the importance of trade within the colony. Matters soon came to a head; Cadillac was recalled, and he left America for good on May 22, 1717. The ex-governor of Louisiana reported his return with his family "very embarrassed for himself and for them till the Board would have the goodness to provide for them." The Regent gave Cadillac permission to come or go as he pleased. Unfortunately, Cadillac chose to rejoin the Court, anxious to defend himself and to intrigue as before. Scarcely arrived in Paris, Cadillac and his oldest son were thrown in the Bastille without further ado.

The explanation for this event is lost in conjecture. The most common view is that the Company of the West feared the eloquence of this unconventional man who had had the audacity to write shortly before his departure from Louisiana that "the Louisiana colony is a monster which has no form of government," and that he had never seen a more wretched country. In order to sustain the credit of the new trading company, it was therefore prudent and urgent to put him in the shadows for a while. This hypothesis is reasonable but not satisfying because it does not explain why his son was also imprisoned.We think that they wished to punish this young officer who had left Louisiana against the wishes of the new governor and at the same time to strike at his father who was accused of having instigated this breach of discipline. In fact, shortly before their embarkation, M. de Lespinay had received orders to "encourage M. de Lamothe's son to remain in the colony in order to lead an expedition to the exact location of the silver and iron mines that his father and he had discovered in the Illinois."

Father and son remained in jail for almost five months, until the gates of the Bastille finally opened on February 8, 1718. As a precautionary measure, the Company of the West relieved Cadillac's oldest son of his Louisiana lieutenancy.

In his misfortune, Cadillac found satisfaction in regaining the friendship of his protectors in the Ministry of Marine and even gained favor with the Duke of Orléans. He reminded them of his salary as governor "from May 5, 1712, when he was named to the post, until the end of

29

10. Castelsarrasin in the 17th century. A 1905 watercolor reconstruction by the architect Émile Gibert. (Original: Burton Historical Collection)

December 1716." Thanks to his supplications to the Regent, he collected his salary—although recalled—until the month of September, 1718. Finally the Cross of Saint-Louis was bestowed on him in recognition of his thirty years of loyal service in the New World. From the evidence available it appears that the Court wished to demonstrate that his misfortune was the consequence of a conflict of a strictly business nature, that it was a question of settling accounts, in no way reflecting upon the honor and the ability of the Governor of Louisiana. Cadillac was a victim of the confusion of administrative functions and commercial interests that he had undoubtedly treasured as long as he enjoyed Crozat's confidence, because it allowed him to pursue his own interests.

Toward the end of 1718, Cadillac and his family settled in St. Nicolas-de-la-Grave. It was the occasion for litigation to settle his parents' inheritance. The inventory of their estate at this time mentioned a "ruinous" house in Caumont, his father's native village, some meadowland at Angeville, some property at St. Nicolas, including the house on the town square where Cadillac was born—now on the point of ruin—and an enclosure with dovecote. On December 14, 1718, his nephews, Jean and Antoine Lasserre, appointed Cadillac as their deputy in all their rights as heirs by which the entire estate at St. Nicolas-de-la-Grave acceded to him.

With the money he obtained through the sale of his property in Detroit to the Canadian Jacques Baudry de Lamarche, Cadillac acquired the office of governor of the town of Castelsarrasin as well as the commission of king's mayor. Except for the levying of tax, the governor played no role in the municipal life of Castelsarrasin, which he apparently seldom visited. For unknown reasons, he was no longer governor at the time of his daughter Marie-Thérèse's marriage, which he did not attend.

Three heirs shared his estate on his death: his oldest son Joseph, François, and Marie-Thérèse. His widow lived with the son François as long as he remained single, until September 10, 1744. Lacking male descendents in the following generations, the name of Lamothe Cadillac disappeared in the St. Nicolas region. There is no record of the inheritance of any property in St. Nicolas. Cadillac's widow had sold some, but the greater part undoubtedly went into the dowry of Marie-Thérèse. Like her parents, this daughter was buried in Castelsarrasin in the Carmelite church.

René Toujas

Cadillac's Career in its Historical Setting

Frank R. Place

To assess the importance of any figure from the past it is important to understand the historical setting, and this is particularly true of Cadillac. He arrived in the New World sometime around 1683. His career roughly coincides with what some older Canadian historians have termed the "Thirty Years War," which began with the renewed Iroquois offensive against the French settlements in the Saint-Lawrence Valley and ended with the Treaty of Utrecht that brought the wars of Louis XIV to a close. Cadillac was not a major figure in these events, but to understand his career in the New World, it is important to keep the events of this period, both in Canada and in Europe, firmly in mind.[1] As with so many figures of the second rank, Cadillac made himself useful to those who dealt with the pressing issues of the day.

When Cadillac stepped off the ship in Port-Royal to begin his obscure apprenticeship in the New World, events in Europe presented new opportunities and, in the long run, vastly greater problems for Louis XIV. In 1683, the Ottoman Turks launched their last offensive against Europe's eastern frontier. Louis XIV took advantage of this situation to lay siege to Luxemburg and to impose, in 1684, the Truce of Ratisboune which won the German princes' reluctant recognition of his territorial acquisitions of the past five years.

While some have viewed 1684 as the apex of Louis XIV's power, it is equally appropriate to view 1684 as the beginning of a long period of decline that lasted until his death in 1715. The defeat of the Turks before the walls of Vienna in September 1683 by a combined force of Germans and Poles with a sprinkling of volunteers from every country in Europe opened the way to a change in the power balance of eastern and central Europe. After some false starts and early setbacks, the German-imperial army, led by Louis XIV's arch rival, the Hapsburg Leopold I of Austria, steadily pushed back the Turks until in 1688 they conquered Belgrade. Never again did the central European states need fear a Turkish invasion. The significance of the German victories was not lost on the French, and as the decade wore on they found themselves confronted by the increasingly hostile, well-armed and assertive German princes intent upon reversing the verdict of 1684. In the face of German resistance the French reacted in the only way they knew how—by further aggression—which only produced greater hostility among the Germans. Louis XIV did for the Germans what they had been unable to do for themselves—create an effective unity under the leadership of the Habsburg emperor.

Central Europe was not the only problem confronting the French. In fact, as Louis XIV found himself drawn into a confrontation with the Germans on his eastern frontier, his interests more and more shifted westward and southward. Particularly, from the mid-80s on he showed renewed concern over the fate of the Spanish empire should, as seemed certain, the feeble Charles II die childless. With its holdings stretching from Italy to the Philippines and including the vast New World empire, Spain could not hope to control its fate free from outside interference. The Spanish holdings in Italy and the affinity between Habsburg Spain and Habsburg Austria made Leopold an interested party. Louis XIV also had family connections and claims on the Spanish inheritance. The Spanish Low Countries, the Mediterranean possessions, and the vast overseas holdings insured that the Maritime Powers, England and the Netherlands, would demand a say in the Spanish succession. Unfortunately, the French efforts to reorient their policy were hindered by the growing hostility against France that existed in practically every European capital. The one exception to this generalized hostility was England. When James II succeeded his brother, Charles II, on the English throne in 1685, he quickly took steps to reintroduce Catholicism. To do so required the circumvention of laws enacted by Parliament specifically to exclude Catholics from a role in government, and James' efforts were widely regarded as an assault on the English constitution. The growing opposition at home forced James into a not entirely welcome dependence upon the friendship and support of France.

Canada, while far removed from these events, nonetheless felt the consequences of Louis XIV's increasingly difficult situation in Europe. French policy toward Canada, particularly after the death in 1683 of the great minister, Jean Baptiste Colbaert, was one of drift. His son and successor, Seignelay, was certainly not the man his father was, but he also had many other matters to deal with at a time when French resources were badly strained.[2] As the 1680s progressed, it had become increasingly apparent that France was badly overextended and that her resources were inadequate to her commitments. In this situation, Seignelay was unable to send the men and supplies needed to protect French settlers from the Iroquois raids and to destroy their power. Moreover, the ultimate enemy was the English colonist, and Louis XIV's need for James' friendship dictated against any action in America that would alienate James or further weaken his position in England. So, efforts to strengthen the colony's hold in North America were postponed until a later time when circumstances were much less favorable to the French.

Cadillac was tucked away in Acadia during this time and was for the most part removed from the pressing events of the day either in Canada or in Europe. However, his time was not spent idly. He established his reputation in several respects during these years. By the end of the decade he was known as a quarrelsome, contentious troublemaker, and as a man not above trading brandy to the Indians. Neither attribute set him apart from large numbers of his contemporaries, but he had also won a reputation as an intelligence expert from his travels and observations in New England and New York. Each of these elements of his reputation played a part in getting him to France and finding a place for himself in the mainstream of French colonial policy for the next twenty or more years. When he was asked to sail on the *Embuscade* in 1689 to gather intelligence along the New England coast, it was because of his knowledge of the area and also quite probably because the governor of Acadia saw an opportunity to rid himself of a troublemaker. Fierce winter storms drove them far out into the Atlantic, and the *Embuscade* eventually reached Franch in the last days of 1689. Cadillac immediately set out for Paris where in the months that followed he established himself with officials of the Ministry of the Marine. In the minds of some officials both his knowledge of the English colonies and his eager participation in the brandy trade stood him in good stead.

The crucial figure in Cadillac's life at this point was Jean-Baptiste de

Lagny who was in charge of the ministry's bureau of commerce and who in effect controlled Canadian affairs. He also had invested in a variety of business ventures and is an interesting example of the combination of government service and capitalist activity which was common in government circles. Recognizing the darker side of Cadillac's character as well as his value in any future military ventures against the English colonies, de Lagny became his protector. Quite likely he saw Cadillac's avid interest in making money as a positive quality. De Lagny was a close friend and collaborator of the Comte de Frontenac who had recently been returned to Canada for his second tour as governor. During his first stay in Canada from 1672 to 1682, Frontenac was mainly noted for his extension of military posts into the interior. These posts had naturally attracted the fur trade and had in effect transformed French policy toward the western regions. As the protector of and collaborator with LaSalle and others, Frontenac had created a permanent French presence in the west to rival that of the Jesuit missionaries. Under the protection of de Lagny and Frontenac, Cadillac took his place among those servants of the crown who combined royal service with participation in the highly profitable fur trade at the western posts.

Cadillac's arrival in France had come at a time when events in Europe were forcing a major reassessment in the thinking of the French court. Hoping to deal a quick knock-out blow that would free him to deal with other, more pressing matters, Louis XIV had sent his armies into Germany in September 1688. The Germans were better armed and resisted more fiercely than the French had thought possible. Moreover, events in England had taken a dramatic turn which spelled trouble for France. The birth of a Catholic heir to James II had created what many prominent Englishmen regarded as the intolerable prospect of a Catholic dynasty ruling England. Waiting in the wings for this opposition to coalesce around him was James' Protestant son-in-law, William of Orange, the *Statholder* of the Netherlands. In October 1688, the "Protestant winds" blew and William sailed for England. Instead of the prolonged civil war the French had expected, William quickly rallied the country to him, and James was forced to spend the rest of his days in French exile. In 1689, William took the lead in the formation of the Grand Alliance which brought together the emperor, the German princes, Spain, the Netherlands, and England in a war against France. Louis XIV found himself fighting a war on all sides against the major states of Europe. The War of the League of Augsburg as it was called dragged on until 1697 and marked the first serious check of the Louis reign.

These events had considerable bearing on the situation in Canada. While war in Europe only worsened the strain on French resources, it did clarify the situation in North America. The English were clearly identified as the enemy and could be dealt with accordingly—keeping in mind the meager resources available to the French in Canada. The Anglo-French rivalry in North America took on added weight in light of the eventuality of a conflict over the Spanish succession. In a struggle for the Spanish lands, control over the Great Lakes and the Mississippi Valley would be vital to the French, for they would provide a link between Canada and Mexico.

Although a clear-cut imperial policy was not yet apparent, the war increased the size and number of garrisons in the western lands. This led to an increase in the fur trade and in the opportunities for profit to those who manned the posts.

Such was the situation in late 1690 when Cadillac returned to Canada. He shortly abandoned Acadia and moved to Quebec where he entered Frontenac's entourage. Armed with the protection of Frontenac and de Lagny, his career began to prosper, and in 1694 he was named military governor of the post at Michilimackinac. The next three years set the pattern for his New World career. He made a lot of money and argued bitterly with nearly everyone he met. His disputes with the Jesuits were legion, but he also was involved in bitter lawsuits with some of the *coureurs de bois* who carried on the fur trade with the Indians. Generally, the protection of Frontenac and de Lagny served to divert or blunt the attacks on Cadillac. Indeed, Frontenac provoked constitutional crisis by his efforts to defend Cadillac against the claims of Louis Durand and Joseph Moreau whose property he had confiscated while at Michilimackinac.

Frontenac and Cadillac had more than de Lagny in their corner. Frontenac was well connected at court, and his kinsmen the Comtes de Pontchartrain, father and son, directed the Ministry of Marine following the death of Colbert de Seignelay in November 1690. Jérôme, the son, was active from the start and by 1696 he was in all but name the secretary of state for marine.[3] For Cadillac and Frontenac, this was both good and bad. On the one hand, Pontchartrain embarked on an expansionist policy which gave greater scope to their money making schemes. On the other, Jérôme kept a close eye on Canadian affairs, and de Lagny no longer had the free hand that he had had before. Interestingly, Cadillac found it advisable to settle the claims of Durand and Moreau before he sailed for France to sell his Detroit scheme.

Cadillac reached France at the end of 1698 and quickly set about to win support for a settlement at Detroit. He had developed his plan while at Michilimackinac. Because of the opposition of the Montreal merchants and most of the Canadian officials, his only hope was to convince Pontchartrain of its advantages. Detroit, according to Cadillac, offered three compelling advantages. By controlling the fur trade, he argued that the glut of furs could be reduced and the French fur market revived. He further argued that by gathering the western tribes at Detroit he could maintain peace among them and ensure their loyalty to France. Finally, he maintained that the French garrison supported by their Indian allies would keep the English and the Iroquois in check. The moment was auspicious. The French had begun their Louisiana venture with a settlement on Mobile Bay, and Pontchartrain was concerned to protect communications between Canada and the Gulf of Mexico against the English and their Indian allies. Armed with the minister's support, Cadillac was able, not without difficulty, to overcome the opposition in Canada and establish his settlement at Detroit. Opposition to the post continued among the Canadians, and it owed its existence to Pontchartrain who saw Detroit as an important element of his imperial strategy.

Cadillac's stay at Detroit provides what is in many ways a melancholy story. Frontenac had died in 1699 while Cadillac was in Paris. Under the watchful eye of Pontchartrain, de Lagny faded into the background, and Cadillac's conduct was subject to sharper scrutiny. Worse, Detroit failed to live up to his claims. The Indians were reluctant to settle there, and the allied tribes fell to fighting among themselves. Cadillac did reduce the flow of furs to Montreal but only by trading with the English and the Iroquois. This, of course, jeopardized Pontchartrain's imperial scheme and tended to produce the very results it was intended to prevent. Moreover, Cadillac's efforts to gain the trade monopoly at Detroit for himself produced unending bickering and complaints. Increasingly disillusioned, Pontchartrain sent out the sieur de Clairambault d'Aigremont to investigate and report on the situation at Detroit. D'Aigremont spent nineteen days in the summer of 1708 at Detroit and sent back a report that was devastating in its criticisms of Cadillac.

It was only a matter of time before Cadillac would be relieved. Pontchartrain had made Detroit his project and a pretext had to be found that would minimize his embarrassment in dropping the man who had created and forwarded the plan. The vacant governorship of Louisiana provided the pretext. On November 3, 1710, Pontchartrain notified Cadillac of his appointment and ordered him to go forthwith to his new post by the overland route. Always aware that his talents could be displayed at the Court, Cadillac delayed, disobeyed his orders, and in 1711 sailed for France. Once in Paris, he made himself of service once more in using his powers of persuasion to entice the financier, Antoine Crozat, to invest heavily in the Louisiana project. He succeeded, but his four years as governor of Louisiana only added a turbulent epilogue to an already turbulent career.

In looking back on the nearly thirty-five years that Cadillac spent in the New World, it becomes clear how much his career depended upon the protection and support of Paris. With the noteworthy exception of Frontenac, Cadillac had no important supporters in Canada, and Frontenac himself depended upon his own connections at the French court. At a time when events in Europe had forced Louis XIV and his ministers to look upon Canada in a new light—as part of an imperial struggle with vast implications both for Europe and America—Cadillac applied his persuasive skills and his grasp of the strategic requirements of an imperial policy to win the favor of important people in the French government. With their support he was able to play his role in the establishment of the European presence in America.

Notes

1. For the reader who desires further background information, I recommend any of the works of W. J. Eccles and particularly his *France in America* (New York, 1972).
2. Donald G. Pilgrim, "France and New France: Two Perspectives on Colonial Security," *Canadian Historical Review*, LV (1974): 381-407.
3. John C. Rule, "Jérôme Phélypeaux, Comte de Pontchartrain and the Establishment of Louisiana, 1696-1715," in *Frenchmen and French Ways in the Mississippi Valley*, ed. Francis McDermott (Urbana, 1969), 178-197.

The Annals of Antoine Laumet de Lamothe Cadillac

Dramatis Personae

D'Auteuil, Ruette: Procurer-general of the High Council in France.

Baudry de Lamarche, Jacques: A Parisian, born in September, 1676. He purchased Cadillac's property rights in Detroit, but his claims were challenged by Rigaud and de Tonti. He served as an attorney in France. He died sometime after 1738.

Beauharnais: Three brothers of this family served in New France. François de Beauharnais, born in 1665, was appointed intendant of New France April 1, 1702. He held this position until he returned to France in 1705; he died in 1746. Charles served as governor-general, and the third brother, born in 1674, was named Claude.

Bienville, Jean Baptiste le Moyne, sieur de: Born in February, 1680. Served on and off as governor of the colony of Louisiana between 1706 and 1740. He died March 7, 1768, in France.

De Bourgmont: Replaced de Tonti as lieutenant to Cadillac at Detroit, 1706, for a short period.

Bouvart, Father Martin (Samuel): A Jesuit, born in Chartres, France, in August 15, 1637, he came to serve in New France on September 30, 1673, eventually becoming superior of the Jesuit mission in the New World. He died in Quebec, August 10, 1705.

Callière, Louis Hector de (sometimes: Callières): Born 1646, he came to Canada to serve as governor of Montreal; later, in 1699, he succeeded Frontenac as governor-general of New France, holding the post until his death in Quebec in 1703.

Carheil, Father Etienne de: Born in France, November, 1633, he received his ordination before coming to Quebec in 1666. He served the Iroquois mission at Cayuga, and then at Michilimackinac from 1687 to 1703. He died in Quebec July 27, 1726.

Chambalon, Louis: Merchant and notary of Quebec, born about 1663, he came to Canada in 1688; died in Quebec, June 15, 1716.

Champigny, Jean Bochart de: Born about 1659, he served as intendant of Canada from 1686 to 1702. He hoped to succeed Frontenac in 1698, but Callière received the appointment as governor-general. He returned to France where he died on September 27, 1720.

Clairambault d'Aigremont, François: He was baptized in France on March 26, 1659; posted as naval commissary at Quebec on September 4, 1701. Pontchartrain recommended him to the intendant Jacques Raudot as an inspector of the western posts which he undertook between June and November, 1708. He became intendant in 1711, holding the post for about a year. He died in Quebec, December 1, 1728.

Dauphin de la Forest, François: Born in Paris about 1649. He served under La Salle at Fort Frontenac (Kingston, Ontario). He came to Detroit in 1705 on Cadillac's recommendation and assumed command of Detroit when Cadillac left. He died in Quebec on October 15, 1714.

Delhalle (de la Halle), Father Bernard Constantin: The parish priest who accompanied Cadillac to Detroit in July, 1701, and founded the church of Ste. Anne at the new post of Detroit. He was slain on July 2, 1706, perhaps accidentally, by an Ottawa bullet in an Indian skirmish, and was buried in his parish grounds.

Deniau, Father Cherubin: He began his seminary studies with the Sulpicians, but was not ordained until five years later in Quebec on December 3, 1700. He arrived in Detroit in August, 1706, to assist Father de la Marche.

Denonville, Jacques René de Brisay, Marquis de: Born in France, he served thirty years in the military before being appointed governor-general of Canada in 1685. A misguided act in 1687 precipitated an unsuccessful war with the Iroquois, forcing him into a humiliating peace treaty in 1688, and his recall to France the next year. He died in 1710.

Dollier de Casson, François: Born in France in 1636, he began his career in the cavalry where he served as captain. He later became a Sulpician missionary and in that role came to Canada in 1666. In 1670, with Father René Brehant de Galinée, he journeyed up the Detroit River and stepped ashore at present-day Detroit someplace between the Rouge River and Fort Wayne. He became Superior of the Montreal mission in 1671, and died on September 25, 1701.

Dugay (Dugué), Jacques: One of the two lieutenants who accompanied Cadillac and de Tonti to Detroit in 1701.

Dulhud (Dulhut), Greyelson: He had been proposed by Denonville in 1686 to found a settlement on the straits between Lake Erie and Lake St. Clair.

Durantaye de l'Espinay (Epinay): Acted as commandant to the Ottawa in 1686.

Enjalran, Father Jean: A Jesuit missionary, born in France on October 10, 1639. Arriving in Quebec, July 22, 1676, he was sent to the St. Ignace missionary. He vigorously opposed Cadillac's plan to have the Ottawas and Hurons of St. Ignace resettled in Detroit. He left Canada in August 1702. He died on February 18, 1718 in France.

Franquelin, Jean Baptiste Louis: A cartographer, born in France about 1651, he went to Canada in 1671. With Cadillac, aboard the *Envieux,* he scouted for the French along the coast of New England and went on with

39

Cadillac to Paris in 1692. The last records of him alive date from France, 1712.

Frontenac, Louis de Baude, Comte de Palluau et de: Born 1620, he died without a surviving child in Quebec on November 28, 1698. He served two terms as governor-general of New France, 1672 to 1682 and 1689 to his death. His disputes with his intendants and with the clergy were responsible for his first recall from office.

Galinée, Father René de Bréhaut de: Born in Brittany, he came to Canada as a Sulpician missionary. He and Father Dollier de Casson began an expedition with La Salle in 1669, but were left on the north shore of Lake Erie. He drew one of the earliest maps of the Great Lakes, and eventually retired to Europe where he died August 15, 1678.

Garnier, Father Charles: One of the first Jesuit missionaries in Michigan, he may have traveled near the Detroit area in 1639. He was killed by the Iroquois when they destroyed the St. Jean Mission, and was canonized in 1930.

Guyon, François: Cadillac engaged in shipping, perhaps privateering, with him in 1687. Probably the uncle of Cadillac's wife.

Guyon, Marie-Thérèse: Wife of Cadillac; daughter of Denis Guyon and Elizabeth Boucher.

La Porte de Louvigny, Louis de: Born in France about 1662, he was appointed commandant of Michilimackinac in 1689. When he returned to France, Cadillac replaced him at that post. Lost at sea August 27, 1725.

Laumet, Antoine: Original name of Cadillac before he assumed the name of Lamothe Cadillac.

Law, John: Scotsman born in 1671; noted economist and financial genius; friend of the regent, the Duke of Orleans; and founder of the French Banque Générale and the Company of the West (Louisiana Company). He triggered a period of inflation; his schemes for the New World exploded as the "Mississippi Bubble" in 1720, forcing him to flee to Italy. Died in 1729.

Lespinay, Jean Michel de: He arrived in Canada in 1687 and was appointed governor of Louisiana following Cadillac on March 12, 1716, perhaps due to his friendship with the financier Crozat. He died in Martinique on January 3, 1721.

Marest, Father Joseph Jacques: Born in France on March 19, 1653, he served as a Jesuit missionary after his arrival in Canada about 1686. Assigned to Michilimackinac in 1688, he argued with Cadillac over the trading of brandy to the Indians.

Ménneval, Louis Alexandre de Friches, Chevalier de: He served as governor of Acadia from 1687 until his surrender to the English in 1690, after which he was sent to England as a prisoner. He died in France in 1709.

Parent, Joseph: Born January 27, 1669, in Quebec. Although it had been thought that he had settled in the area of the future Detroit prior to Cadillac, evidence indicates that he arrived circa 1705 or thereafter.

Péchagut: Family name of Cadillac's mother.

Pontchartrain, Jérôme Phélypeaux, Comte de: Born 1674, he was one of the many public officials of the Phélypeaux family that rose to high office. He served as secretary of state, Department of the Marine, from 1699 until 1715 when he was forced out of office. He died in 1747.

Ramezay, Claude de: Born in 1657, he came to Canada in 1685 and was appointed governor of Montreal May 15, 1704. He was the administrator of New France from 1714 to 1716, dying in Montreal on August 1, 1724.

Raudot, Antoine Denis: Born in 1679, he served as inspector-general of the Marine, administrator of Louisiana, and intendant of New France from 1705 to 1710. He died at Versailles, July 28, 1737.

Raudot, Jacques: Brother of Antoine Denis, born 1647 and died 1728.

Renaud Dubuisson, Jacques Charles: Born in Paris in 1666, he came to Canada in 1685-86. He was appointed interim commandant of Detroit on September 10, 1710, to succeed Cadillac until Dauphin de la Forest, who was ill, was able to take over. Cadillac's continued presence in Detroit after he was relieved caused considerable friction, but Renaud held the post until the summer of 1715. He died at Trois-Rivières in 1739.

Roy, Pierre: A Detroit resident with his Indian wife circa 1702-3. He is sometimes claimed as having lived in the Detroit area before Cadillac's arrival.

Tonti (Tonty), Alphonse de: Second-in-command at Detroit, which he helped to found with Cadillac.

Vaillant de Gueslis, Father François: Born on July 20, 1646, in France, he came to Quebec in 1670 and five years later was inducted into the priesthood. As a Jesuit missionary, he set up the Indian mission in Detroit in 1701, and soon left because of conflict with Cadillac. He returned to France in 1717, where he died the following year on September 24.

Vaudreuil, Philippe de Rigaud, Marquis de: Born in 1643, he arrived in New France in 1687 as commander of the French troops, and was later appointed governor of Montreal in 1698. On the death of Callière, he became the administrator of the government of Canada, then lieutenant-governor and governor in 1705, the post he held until his death in Quebec on October 10, 1725.

In this year of 1658, on the 10th day of the month of March, in the parish church of St. Nicolas-de-la-Grave, I, Jean Boscus, curé, have baptized the child born on the 5th day of this month, to whom has been given the name Antoine Laumet, son of M. Jean Laumet, lawyer of the Court, and of Jeanne de Péchagut, his wife. Acting as godfather, Antoine Péchagut; and as godmother, Anne de Gibrac.

(Baptismal Record, Archives,
St. Nicolas-de-la-Grave)

The family holdings of "Les Laumets" have suggested that Cadillac was born there, and not in St. Nicolas-de-la-Grave:

Antoine Laumet was born in a hamlet named les Laumets near Caumont after his family.

(DCB)

There is no evidence to support this supposition except the fact of the name and property. On the other hand, it is most usual that the child be baptized in the village of his birth, rather than carried to a different parish for the rite.

The Village of St. Nicolas-de-la-Grave

St. Nicolas-de-la-Grave was founded in 1135 by Guillaume, the abbot of Moissac, with the concurrence of Saxet, Viscount of Lomagne, and of Sybille, Viscountess of Auvillat. In the 13th century, the rights of the Viscounts of Lomagne were bought back, and the abbots of Moissac remained sole lords of St. Nicolas. There they built a chateau in which the Abbot Aymeric de Peyrac wrote his chronicles of Moissac at the end of the 14th century. A riot of day-labor farmers occurred in 1793 and the town remained republican during the royalist insurrection.

The porch and the octagonal bell tower of the church are in the Toulousian style, built about 1685; the portal comes from the beginning of the 17th century. Inside the church is the seat of St. Ansbert, the 17th-century celebrated abbot of Moissac.

The chateau of the abbots of Moissac, which legend attributes to Richard the Lion-Hearted, was constructed in the 13th century and remodeled in the 19th century. Little remains of the chateau that Aymeric de Peyrac occupied.

(Méras, *Tarn*)

A Visit to the Home of Cadillac

C. M. Burton

One of the objects I had in going to France in the winter of 1906-7 was to visit the birthplace of Cadillac and personally to inspect the home and surroundings of the man who is so prominently connected with the early history of America . . . .

On the 6th of February, 1907, Mrs. Burton and I started from Paris by an early train, and reached Montauban the same evening. This city is 31

The Annals of Antoine Laumet de Lamothe Cadillac

1658

March 5—Antoine Laumet, who later adopts the name of Lamothe Cadillac, born in St. Nicolas-de-la-Grave, Department of Tarn-et-Garonne, in the house of his maternal grandfather on "rue de Faure," near the public square.

March 10—Antoine Laumet presented for baptism by his maternal grandfather Antoine Péchagut and grandmother Anne de Gibrac.

11. The church in St. Nicolas-de-la-Grave where Cadillac was baptized. From a 1905 watercolor by Alphonse Fauré, a drawing teacher in Montauban. (Original: Burton Historical Collection)

miles from the city of Toulouse so often referred to in Cadillac's correspondence. Montauban is in the department of Tarn-et-Garonne on the River Tarn, and contains about 30,000 people. It is a very old city, founded in the 12th century, and was one of the early strongholds of the Albigeneses, the French Protestants. Notwithstanding its subjugation to the powers of the Catholic Church, a few years before the birth of Cadillac, it retained a great following of religious reformers. These men submitted to the open observance of adherence to the church while they practiced in private a larger freedom of religious thought. The entire country was imbued with the principle of religious freedom and the people so continued to think, even after the outward observance of Protestantism was denied them, and many of them now retain the religious opinions of their Albigensian ancestors.

No one can read the voluminous correspondence of Cadillac without observing that, although he was a good Catholic churchman, he was a protestant against the impositions of the Jesuits and the tyranny of the Church as imposed by that order.

It was in the neighborhood of Montauban that Cadillac was born and passed his early youth and old age, and near here his remains were buried.

Our first visit was the home of the Chanoine Fernand Pottier, President of the Archeological Society. He was not at his home when we called, but the attendant asked us to step in and wait a few moments for him . . . . I was quite prepared to meet a student and was not surprised, when a little while later, the Chanoine (or canon) of the Catholic Church came in and introduced himself to me. He is a very pleasant little old gentleman, probably 70 years of age, and as we discovered, the idol of the village, for everyone seemed to think very much of him and appeared to love him as if he was in reality, as he was spiritually, the father of the community. On learning our errand, he at once set about entertaining us. He first took us to the office of Mr. Edouard Forestie, printer and lithographer. Here I found some twelve or more volumes in manuscript, containing the records of the district of Tarn and Garonne from 1527 to 1620. These books were once in the custody of Jean Laumet, the father of Cadillac. He was the judge of the court of the district and it was his duty to examine these records and certify to the possession of them. His name is endorsed, officially, on each of the volumes. Mr. Forestie is carefully examining the books for the purpose of extracting new data relative to the Laumet family. He has prepared a book for his own use, in which he has devoted a page to each year of Cadillac's life and, as he has been working at it for several years, his book is filled with interesting material.

I spent a considerable part of the day with these old volumes and in conversation with several members of the Archaeological Society who called at the office. According to a previous arrangement with the Chanoine we returned to his home in the afternoon, where we met another and younger priest, about thirty-eight years of age, professor of English, in the seminary of Montauban. Although the general conversation was Cadillac and his family, the host took pains to entertain us with other matters connected with their village . . . .

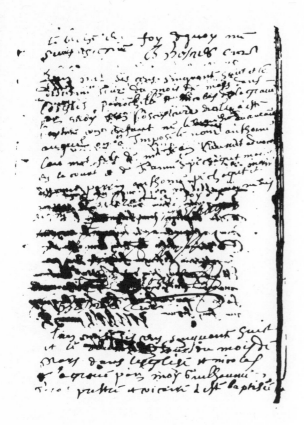

12. The Baptismal Record of Antoine Laumet (de Lamothe Cadillac) of 1658.

On the third floor of the priest's house was a large room used for the meetings of the Archaeological Society. On one side of this room was a canvas on which were displayed many interesting pictures illustrating the trip of the members of this society to Moissac and St. Nicolas-de-la-Grave in 1904, to place a tablet at the birthplace of Cadillac. They had pictures of the home, the church, the chateau, and the street in the little village and several pictures of the journey to Castelsarrasin, where Cadillac spent the last years of his life. The evening was passed very pleasantly with a large company all intent on making our stay as interesting as possible, and when we parted, it was to make preparation for an early start for Moissac in the morning.

Moissac is a railroad station about seventeen miles from Montauban and we reached the place very early the next day, February 8. Here we took a carriage and rode six miles to St. Nicholas-de-la-Grave. The country through which we rode is very beautiful. The district of Tarn-et-Garonne derives its name from the two rivers Tarn and Garonne that serve as feeders to the great canals Midi and Lateral that connect the Atlantic Ocean with the Mediterranean Sea. Montauban is situated on the Tarn, while Moissac, a city of about 90,000 inhabitants, is located on the Garonne. Our road to St. Nicolas-de-la-Grave for a distance ran parallel to the river and high above its banks. Below us on the left we could see the winding stream, and beyond the river the great stretch of fertile farm lands in the distance, while behind us rose the hills that shut out our view from the north. Crossing the stream on a high bridge, a ride of little more than an hour brought us to the village of St. Nicolas-de-la-Grave, the birthplace of Cadillac, before nine o'clock in the morning. Our first call was at the home of the village physician. This gentleman took the utmost interest in our visit. He devoted himself to us during the time spent in the village. We first visited the house which was the birthplace of Cadillac. It is a one-story brick dwelling about five hundred years old, I was informed. In the part of the building are two or three large living rooms. Behind these rooms is a small court and on one side of the court is a part of the building two stories in height, used now for sleeping apartments. The ceilings of the rooms are very high, and whatever heat is needed is derived from fireplaces in the living rooms. Although it was in the middle of the winter when we made our visit, and the weather was as cold as it is usually in that region, we found roses in bloom in the open air in the courtyard I have mentioned.

The street in front of the dwelling is about twenty-five feet in width, paved with cobble stones. In the neighborhood are many other dwellings of similar size and antiquity, while occasionally a newer and larger building has been erected. The Cadillac building now belongs to Louis Ayral, a lawyer in Paris, and is occupied by his mother who kindly led us through the various rooms and pointed out the portions of interest.

On the eighth of November, 1904, the Archaeological Society of Tarn and Garonne placed a tablet on this building in honor of the noted man whose birthplace it was. Translated, the inscription on the tablet reads: "To the memory of Antoine Laumet de Lamothe Cadillac, born in this house March 5, 1658, colonizer of Canada and Louisiana, founder of Detroit, Governor of Castelsarrasin, where he died in 1730."

13. The Romanesque Cloister of the Abbey Church of St. Pierre in Moissac, the seat of the powerful abbots who supported the Laumet family.

14. "In the year 1904, on Tuesday, the 8th of November, a hundred or so members of the Archaeological Society of Tarn-et-Garonne, led by their president, the Canon Pottier, returned to St. Nicolas-de-la-Grave, the birthplace of Antoine de Lamothe Cadillac to solemnly inaugurate a commemorative plaque to be placed on the natal house of the great colonizer of the Great Lakes region of North America." (Drawing of the plaque and the opening lines from the volume "Hommage de la Société archéologique de Tarn-et-Garonne à la ville de Détroit.")

1676

The only record of Cadillac's youth in Gascony, after his baptism, and before he is found in the New World, is the possible reference of an "A. Laumet" who signed as one of the witnesses on the marriage contract of a cousin of Cadillac.

1677

After the death of his parents, Antoine Laumet enters the military. He is appointed a cadet in the regiment of Dampierre-Lorraine. Subsequently, he is promoted to lieutenant in the regiment of Clairambault (Claembault) and is garrisoned in Paris.

1683

Antoine Laumet sails from France for Canada. Antoine Laumet settles in Port-Royal, Acadia (currently Annapolis Royal, Nova Scotia).

St. Nicholas is a small village, containing two or three thousand people. It is as we reckon time, very old. The streets and houses have changed but little in the two hundred and fifty years since Cadillac's birth, and every street of the village has borne the impress of his childish feet. Here stands the little church where he was baptized, whose archives contain the record of his birth and that of his brothers and sisters. Here he attended church as a youth, received his first communion, and drank in such words of religious liberty as were current. Nearby is the old chateau, now used, in part, for a school for boys. The children were at recess in the play yard when we called. They were all nicely and cleanly dressed in the peculiar garb of the children of this section, and all wore wooden shoes or *sabots*, while at play, over their slippers or low leather shoes.

Did Antoine Laumet serve in the military? The mention of this regiment in which he is supposed to have served occurs in one of Cadillac's memorials written forty-three years after the date when he supposedly began his military career . . . . this rank [of lieutenant] is one of the many honors conferred by Cadillac upon himself . . . . the official Acadian correspondence contains no allusion to his ever having held any rank in the army.

(Delanglez, "Early Years")

As for his claim to have held a commission in the French Army, it is almost invalidated by the contradictory statements he made about his rank and regiment. In 1690 he told a clerk of the Ministry of Marine that he had been an infantry captain; the following year he informed Frontenac that he had held the rank of lieutenant in the Regiment Clairambault; in a memorial of the mid 1720s to the Ministry of Marine he demoted himself to a cadet in the Régiment de Dampierre-Lorraine.

(DCB)

However, Dr. Henri Négrié, who had access to the archival records for his study of Cadillac, maintains that Cadillac served in the Clairambault Regiment that debarked France for the New World.

The Transatlantic Trip by Sail

During this period of sailing ships, sea voyages were always of long duration. Return trips, from America to France, were relatively easy because of the winds from the West, but this was not true of out-going voyages, which were necessarily longer because one had to sail rather far South, near the latitude of the Azores, to catch the tradewinds which blew from East to West and let them carry the ships to the first landfalls. After arriving near the Bahamas, the ships joined the Gulf Stream and at a distance followed the American coast from South to North up to Chesapeake Bay. There they left the warm current which flowed toward Europe and continued northward to Louisburg in Acadia, where, weather allowing, the mouths of the Saint Lawrence emptied into the current coming from Labrador. The boats entered the river, congested with ice in the winter, and put in at last at the foot of Quebec.

(Négrié, ''Pioneer'')

This change of name in New France, from Laumet to Lamothe, and then later with the addition of ''Cadillac,'' has been viewed as both innocent and evil, as a practical diversion to help a young adventurer to get ahead in a new world, and as a devious falsification to cloak a criminal record in the land of his birth.

But, what's in a name . . . .?
    In the early official reports he is referred as ''young LaMothe'' possibly because he had relatives by that name or, possibly because La Mothe was a name identified with the area from which he came. I have found five towns near St. Nicolas-de-la-Grave that had the word ''La Mothe'' as part of their names. The name was quite common in France and soon he adopted it.

(Simons, ''Cadillac'')

    About the name ''Lamothe'': it is a matter of it being a name applied to a location throughout France . . . . The feudal ''mothe'' was an artificial slope surrounded by a palisade, the ancestor of the fortified chateau of the Middle Ages.

(Méras, *Tarn*)

Professor Philippe Wolff of the University of Toulouse, France, writes that, people, especially of noble condition, used to be called after the location of their home or castle, very often at least. This is why, as a family name, you will find 'de la Motte' (or Mothe) recur again and again, without any relation between all these cases . . . . As to Cadillac, there is no sin in taking the title, even if it was not quite legal. Many people did it and, after two or three generations, their descendants were considered as true nobles. Had Cadillac been more successful, there would have been no fuss about his title.

A modern example may illustrate the point: President Giscard-d'Estaing's family name was Giscard for many years. In 1922, his father, for personal reasons, legally changed the family name to ''Giscard d'Estaing,'' evidently to honor the illustrious ancestor Admiral Charles Henri, Count d'Estaing, who had fought in the American Revolution. The president of France is the great-great grandson of the admiral whose name, ''d'Estaing,'' was taken from the locality bearing that name, in Rouergue, from which the family more or less came.
    Although Cadillac undoubtedly had a solid education and possessed a certain amount of culture, he had no desire to follow his father's career. To be a small town lawyer, a judge at St. Nicolas, is not what

In written reports, Antoine Laumet is for the first time referred to as ''young Lamothe.''

15. An early 20th-century view of Castelsarrasin. The octagonal bell tower of the parish church is in the background. The name of the city probably is derived from its early chateau which was built on the model of Saracen architecture. Thus ''Castellum Sarracenum.''

47

16. Cadillac's birthplace decorated for the 1901 celebration.

interested him. An adventurous spirit, he wanted to become an officer and to serve abroad, but to obtain this end, especially if he hoped to gain a position commensurate with his ambitions, he had to gain access to the noble class; since Laumet smacked too much of common origins, he had to change his name. But what name? He finally arrogated to himself another name with noble connotations, Lamothe Cadillac, which, with a flourish, would make him a true son of Gascony.

Where did he find this imaginary name? We know that while still a child he attended the baptism of a little cousin whose godmother was Mme. Malenfont, the wife of Sylvestre de Lamothe, a counsellor in the high court of Toulouse. This man, who died in 1684 in Toulouse, was lord of Bardiques and of Moutet, neighboring parishes of St. Nicolas, and perhaps was related to the Laumet family.

The origin of the name Cadillac is more difficult to discover. One can presume that he also borrowed this from his circle, a relative or friend.

Indeed, without looking further afield in the Bordelais, for example, where Cadillac is a well-known place name which might have attracted him during a trip, we must keep in mind the following facts.

First, one finds in the memoirs of Sieur de Pontis, a captain in the Royal Army under Louis XIII who participated in the siege of Montauban in 1621, the name of a hamlet or locality called Cadillac situated near Montech, consequently nearer to St. Nicolas. But this place has disappeared, for it does not figure on any map of the general staff. Several skirmishes occurred there when the army, retiring from Montauban, was attacked by a group of Hugenists before Montech, which Pontis successfully defended.

On the other hand, it is also possible that this name was used for the locality even during the lifetime of Antoine Laumet. At any rate, in 1693, during the Terror, there lived at Saint-Aignan, near Castelsarrasin and a few leagues from St. Nicolas, one Antoine Cadillac, a brewer, who together with one Marie Cadillac—perhaps his wife—and a Guillaume Laumet, is inscribed in the registers of the local Popular Society as an ardent Jacobin.

So Cadillac was able to appropriate a new name without too much difficulty. We should not be astonished at this deceit. Such substitutions were a common practice at that time. One of the future officers in the regiment of Marine, Delpéré, took the name Cadillac; and under this name he made his career, even becoming a Knight of Saint Louis. Although the illustrious explorer La Salle, does the same, this will not prevent him from receiving patents of nobility from the king. The royal government, whose treasury was often empty, not only tolerated such activity, but willingly confirmed it for financial considerations, especially when it was justified by outstanding service.

Yet . . . Cadillac lacked a coat of arms. From where did he take them? From the family Esparbès de Lussau, from the Chateau of Lamothe at Bardiques. He shamelessly appropriated their blazon (with the first and fourth quarters sand colored and the opposites silver, including three blackbirds, two in the second quarter and one in the third quarter, perched on fesses striped with azure), bothering only to change the color of the enamel on the escutcheon.

(Négrié, "Pioneer")

When he married Thérèse Guyon in Quebec in 1687, he was inscribed on the register as "Antoine de Lamothe, Esquire, Sieur de Cadillac . . . son of Mr. Jean de la Mothe, sieur of the place called Cadillac of Launay and Semontel, counsellor of the parliament of Toulouse . . . ." Most of this was pure invention. His father, Jean Laumet, was a lawyer and petty magistrate of St. Nicolas-de-la-Grave, while his mother was descended from a long line of merchants. There is no evidence to show that the seigniory of Cadillac ascribed to Jean Laumet ever existed. Cadillac, feeling the need of a coat of arms, and not being entitled to any, appropriated the arms of the barons of Lamothe-Bardigues belonging to the family of Esparbes de Lussan. Such pretensions are clearly indicative of a Gascon running true to type. His nimble imagination always embroidered the truth; exaggerations and extravagant statements came natural to him. It is not easy to conceive Cadillac as ever doing anything temperately.

(Paré, *Church*)

17. The towered Chateau of Richard the Lion-Hearted in St. Nicolas-de-la-Grave, built in the 13th and remodeled in the 19th centuries.

With regard to the various names assumed by Cadillac and applied to him by others, though there are some things as yet unexplained, there can be no doubt as to the identity of the person to whom they are applied.

His signature, made at Castelsarrasin 1729, at the time of the marriage of his daughter, harmonizes closely with his signature, written a quarter of a century before, in the records of St. Anne's church in Detroit. The name Lamothe, appended to the registry of marriage at Quebec in 1687, is unlike his later signatures, but changes in form of letters are not at all unusual. The chief trouble with the record of Quebec is that the statement it contains in regard to his father and mother does not harmonize with the facts obtained from France. This, however, may be accounted for by the probability that the record was carelessly taken down, or hurriedly written.

Possibly the intimation which we find in one old manuscript, that Cadillac left France on account of personal difficulties, is true, and if so, this may have been the reason for his change of name . . . .

It was not at all uncommon, at that day, or even in later times, for the same person to be designated by two or more names, entirely different from each other. Laumet was undoubtedly his family name; it was used both by him and his wife, as was also the name La Mothe; and sometimes both names were used in the same document.

When Cadillac's granddaughter was married to Bartholomew Gregoire, at Castelsarrasin, she was styled Marie Thérèse de Laumet de Cadillac. In 1741 and 1742 the French records of transfers of land titles give the name of Cadillac's wife as Madame Thérèse de Guyon, wife of Antoine Laumet de la Mothe Cadillac.

(Farmer, *History*)

18. The Chateau of Richard the Lion-Hearted converted into the city hall and school building of St. Nicolas-de-la-Grave.

I confess that I do not understand how the old French names are made up. It seems to me that prior to the time that Detroit was founded, each of a family, on his attaining his majority, took to himself such a name as he saw fit—possibly taking the name from some tract of land—some seniory that he possessed and named. Thus we have in many instances, a family of brothers each bearing different names. The use of the given name was little known and was scarcely ever employed except in official documents where the individual was referred to as being the son of some person whose full name was given. Even as late as 1700 the use of the surname was not fully understood and it is no infrequent circumstance to find the name of a descendant entirely unlike that of his ancestor.

I call to mind now, a few local names affected by the uncertainty of names, as the family of St. Aubin. The Detroit ancestor of this family was named Casse and the name St. Aubin was attached as a nickname. His children bore the same name of Casse, but as third generation was reached, the name St. Aubin was frequently used alone and the name Casse omitted. Take the family of Beaubien. Their family name was Cuilliere. The Laffertys belong to the family of Vissiere. These are only illustrations. There are many other families in Detroit that have as abruptly and unceremoniously changed their surnames and it needs the constant watch upon each name to be able to trace the families through the generations. Another thing about these early French people that appears odd to us is that the women, upon marriage, did not take the name of their husbands. Wherever a woman is referred to, her maiden name is given, followed by the statement that she is the wife of some person who is named and also frequently followed by the names of her parents. This peculiarity frequently assists one in tracing the identity of names otherwise obscure.

(Burton, *Cadillac*)

1686

French plan to establish a post at the straits.

June—M. Duluth, directed to establish a post on the Detroit River, goes instead to the St. Clair River, near Port Huron, to found Fort Duluth (Fort St. Jospeh).

Extract of a letter from the Marquis de Denonville to M. de la Durantaye, commandant to the Ottawas.

Villemarie, June 6, 1686
. . . I intend to make use of two posts, one at the strait of Lake Erie and the other at the portage of Toronto. I wish the first to be occupied by M. Dulhud, to whom I will give twenty men. I am writing him to be ready to leave for the strait in order to select an advantageous site where he can entrench himself and then put a secure and trustworthy person of his choice as commandant.

Extract of a letter from the Marquis de Denonville to M. Greyelson Dulhud [Dulhut].

Villemarie, June 6, 1686
you will see from the letter I have written to M. de la Durantaye that I intend for you to occupy a post at an advantageous place to insure us this passage . . . .

1687

Cadillac engaged in shipping with François Guyon in Nova Scotia, becomes intimately familiar with conditions of the Atlantic seaboard.

June 25—Cadillac marries Marie-Thérèse Guyon of Beauport, near Quebec.

Marriage Document

On the 25th of the month of June, in the year 1687, after the betrothal and the publication of two banns of marriage, having obtained dispensation of the third from M. de Bernieres, vicar-general of the Lord

Bishop of Quebec, the first having been published the 22nd and the second on the 24th of the current month, between Antoine de Lamothe, sieur de Cadillac of the village of Port Royal in Acadia, aged about twenty-six years, son of M. Jean de la Mothe, sieur of the place named Cadillac of Launay and Semontel, counsellor of the parliament of Toulouse, and of Mme. Jeanne de Malenfant, his father and mother, of the first part; and of Marie-Thérèse Guyon, daughter of the deceased Denis Guyon, a citizen of this place, and of Elizabeth Boucher, her father and mother, of the second part, aged about seventeen years; and not finding any hinderance, I, François Dupré, curé of this parish, have solemnly married and given the nuptial benediction in the presence of the following witnesses, sieurs Berthelmi Desmarest, Michel Denis Guyon, Jacques Guyon, Denis le Maitre, who have signed along with the husband and wife.

Demarest

Françoise Dupré

Lamothe Launay

Marie-Thérèse Guyon

Jacques Guyon

Michel Guyon

Denis le Maitre

The family of Marie-Thérèse Guyon, originally from Perche, had been in Canada for a generation. Not only does Cadillac adopt in his marriage document his "new" names and family, but he also changes his age from almost 30 to "about 26."

Cadillac's Land Grant:
A grant of two leagues with an island of fourteen leagues, over which he had the right to administer high, middle, and low justice, on which bordered the sea and the banks of the Duaquec (Douaguek) River.
[*Today the Union River in the State of Maine, opposite Port Royal in Acadia, the island of Mount Desert and Bar Harbor.*]

Cadillac describes himself to the Minister of Marine as:
the best informed person there is on the country stretching from Acadia south through New England, New Holland until the Carolinas, having made several trips by sea and land and having even traveled 250 leagues into the interior. I have seen the most important places, have examined their fortifications and artillery, and I know pretty well the number of inhabitants and their religious diversity.

(Toujas, *Destin*)

Cadillac, in France, writes to the Minister of Marine, December 29, 1689:
I feel myself obliged to inform you of my trip. MM. de la Caffinière and de Ménneval proposed that I embark on the *Embuscade* for a month's campaign without telling me what I would be doing; they told me only that it was in the service of the King and that I would gain merit with Your Grace. After having cruised to the west for some time, we encountered winds so violent and contrary that it was impossible to make land, and we were

Cadillac and bride return to live in Port Royal.

1688
July 23—Cadillac, through the good offices of a cousin, Gorgas, and a friend named Mirament, obtains a grant of land in Acadia from the Marquis de Denonville.

1689
Having traveled extensively in the English colonies, Cadillac returns to France to provide the ministry with first-hand information on the conditions prevailing along the Atlantic seaboard.

Cadillac, back in New France with his family in Quebec, begins friendship with Governor Frontenac who had succeeded Denonville.

Cadillac is appointed lieutenant in the colonial troops.

Sent by Frontenac to cruise off the coast of Acadia, in a defensive move against the British, Cadillac's ship is forced by storm out to sea and, then proceeds on to land in France.

1692

Cadillac, back in France again, is interviewed by Count de Pontchartrain. Cadillac presents his plans for the defense of Canadian rivers and lakes by means of an armada of light craft.

Cadillac and map maker Jean-Baptiste Franquelin reconnoiter the New England coast.

1694

April 15—Cadillac is appointed by royal decree captain in the marines as well as ensign in the navy.

September 28—Cadillac leaves Montreal for his new assignment.

19. Cadillac's signature. Document signed by Cadillac and Hazeur, dated September 17, 1694.
(Burton Historical Collection)

forced to set sail for Europe, whereas I had been promised that I would be returned to Port Royal.

(Margry, *MetD*)

An historical coincidence: One of the first Counts de Pontchartrain to serve the royal court—Paul Phélypeaux, 1569-1621—one-time secretary of state, had died while fighting the Huguenots at Castelsarrasin where, over a century later, Cadillac was also to die after having served as mayor of the town. This early Count de Pontchartrain was the great-grandfather of Jérôme Phélypeaux de Pontchartrain who supported Cadillac, and after whom Cadillac named the Detroit fort.

On September 16, 1694, Frontenac writes,
Sieur la Porte de Louvigny, commandant of Michilimackinac since 1690, having indicated to me that he must go to France to take care of his affairs there, has our permission to return.

We do not think that a better replacement for him could be made than that of sieur de Lamothe Cadillac, captain of the troops of the detachment of the Marines. On several occasions we have observed his courage, wisdom, experience, and good conduct. In light of these qualities, we have assigned sieur de Lamothe Cadillac as commandant in place of sieur la Porte de Louvigny . . . .

(Margry, *MetD*)

Basically the duties of the commandant were threefold: to keep all the western tribes in the French alliance, to make them live in harmony with each other, and to induce them to wage war relentlessly on the Five Nations. It is quite odd that Frontenac . . . should have asserted that Cadillac was acquitting himself very well in this work when the facts . . . reported proved the exact contrary. Cadillac was unable to prevent the Hurons and Iroquois from exchanging embassies for the purpose of concluding a peace treaty; he was unable to preserve harmony between the various western tribes, much less persuade them to form a large striking force to attack the Iroquois . . . . Cadillac may have been a failure as a commandant but he proved to be very adroit as a fur-trader.

(*DCB*)

Cadillac is pleased with the condition of his new post at Michilimackinac and the prospect before him:
There is a good wooden fort, a garrison of well-disciplined, elite soldiers, and sixty houses forming a long, straight street. Not counting those who actually reside there only two or three months of the year, there are around two hundred men who are choice types, the best turned out in the New World. I do not have a moment's rest; I am in the midst of thirty or thirty-two tribes who are neither civilized nor controlled, enemies of one another, and who make war at a moment's notice. However, it is necessary to manage all those tribes, which is not easy because they are insubordi-

nate. That is, there are almost as many chiefs, almost as many bonnets, as tribes . . . . The commander of this post ought always to keep a watchful eye, ready to deal with anything.

(Toujas, Destin)

Frontenac describes Cadillac as
a man who carries out his duty to the fullest and who is wise, prudent, and perhaps more penetrating than certain people, among whom he must live, would prefer.

(September 4, 1695)

Cadillac writes to Roland de Lagny:
I am so exhausted that I have several times requested permission to leave from Count de Frontenac. I have pressed him to relieve me next year, and I dare to hope that he will no longer refuse me and that he will have the goodness to follow with a request to the Court for my return to France.

Friction between Cadillac and the Jesuits, which had begun before his appointment to Michilimackinac increased as Cadillac wanted the Indians gathered around the post for trading, to be educated by civil authorities, and to be given liquor in trade. The Fathers wanted the Indians missionized by them in place, and to be denied alcohol. Four Jesuit fathers were stationed at St. Ignace, among them Father Carheil, whom Cadillac described as the most violent and seditious person he had ever known. Cadillac reported the following exchange between himself and the Father:

Fr. Carheil told me, one day, that I neither obeyed the orders of the King nor had them obeyed; that I permitted the liquor traffic, and the scandalous relations between Frenchmen and squaws, in defiance of the prohibitions of His Majesty. I answered him that I took orders from my superiors, and that I knew my business too well to change or modify them. He told me that I would have to answer to God, and not to the government, when it commanded me to act against the will of God, and that the permission to engage in the liquor traffic was against His will. The Indians might desire to drink to excess; it was certainly God's will that they be deprived of liquor. I had no right to obey theirs in preference to His. The Indians had no right to liquor for the beaver which they bartered, for it belonged to God who had given it to them for a good purpose. Consequently, when I knew they were using it for an evil purpose, that is for liquor, I should not barter with them no matter what my orders were.

I answered that this was seditious language that smelled of heaven, and I begged him to desist. Again he told me that I was not obeying the orders of the King, and that I was putting on airs, and at the same time he shook his fist under my nose. I tell you, Monsieur, that I almost forgot that he was a priest, and was on the point of breaking his jaw. But, thanks be to God, I contented myself by taking him by the arm, and leading him out of the fort, telling him to stay out of it in the future.

(Paré, Church)

1695
Cadillac begins to trade brandy for beaver pelts with the Indians, contrary to royal decree and church interests.

Father Carheil reproaches Cadillac for his conduct and imperious manner; Frontenac defends his appointee.

1696
Cadillac and the Jesuit missionaries file charges and countercharges. Discouraged by the complaints and by the depressed market for fur skins, Cadillac asks to be relieved of his duties.

20. The "Family Crest" and seal adopted by Cadillac, from a document dated 1695.

May 1—The King orders withdrawal of garrisons from main posts in the West.

1697

August 29—Cadillac returns to Quebec with the pull-back from western posts.

1698

June 13—Frontenac dies in Quebec; he is replaced by Louis Hector de Callière, governor of Montreal.

1699

Cadillac goes to France to argue his case before Pontchartrain for establishing a colony on "the narrows of Lake Huron"; to found a French trading post that will protect French fur trade interests from English encroachment; and to unite the western Indians in one place.

May 27—King Louis XIV informs Callière and the intendant Champigny of his approval of Cadillac's plan and asks them to support it if the design is judged practical.

King grants to Cadillac 15 arpents of land at the site where he will establish the post.

Concerning Cadillac, Frontenac writes to the Minister of Marine:
I can assure you that no one could be more satisfied than I am with the vigilance and good conduct of this officer.

(October 15, 1697)

Frontenac's support of Cadillac in the face of the charges brought by the Jesuit Fathers may be in part the result of his own suspicions concerning the Order. Frontenac writes to the ministry,
To speak frankly, the Jesuits think as much of the conversion of beaver as they do of souls; their missions are for the most part pure mockeries.

Speaking of himself in the third person, Cadillac writes to Pontchartrain:
It seems that up until now Lamothe has not undertaken any task unsuccessfully and this encourages him to commit himself to the following proposals and to see them through to the end, provided the Court accords him the honor of its protection. He well knows that he has enemies, but in this respect he acts like a good traveller who follows his route without turning aside and without stopping at the noise of the yelping creatures who cry after him. He has not tried to please everyone. Provided that his superiors be satisfied with his conduct, he will be satisfied.

(Margry, MetD)

Extract of a memorandum from the King to Callière and Champigny:
                              Versailles, May 27, 1699
    His Majesty sends a memorandum that has been drawn up by sieur de Lamothe Cadillac, containing a proposal to establish all the Indians allied with us in a single group of communities on the land between Lake Erie, the lake of the Hurons, and the lake of the Illinois [Michigan]. The reasons supporting this proposal are explained by sieur de Lamothe Cadillac in his memorandum and need not be repeated here. His Majesty desires that an assembly of leading citizens and the best heads of the land with sieur Lamothe examine this proposal, discuss the reasons for and against the project, and provide His Majesty with a concise report. If it is found good and practical, His Majesty desires that the necessary steps be taken immediately as they will have the permission of His Majesty.

(Margry, MetD)

Extract from the memorandum to the King written by Governor Callière concerning Cadillac's project to establish Detroit.
    I strongly approve of Sr. de Lamothe Cadillac's project, although some matters must be straightened out.
    The location of the post of Detroit certainly should be the most expedient in terms of climate, fertile soil, and living conditions, and it will not be difficult to assemble the Ottawas there, The plan should ultimately be successful, but I find two major difficulties.
    The first problem is the proximity of the Iroquois who will unquestionably be suspicious that the post would interfere with their hunting in a

land that they claim to have conquered, although the truth is that the Ottawas annually hunt there. After due deliberation, I find that this post could very well serve to perpetuate the war among us, our allies, and the Iroquois.

The second difficulty is that because of this same nearness, our Indians might come to trade their beaver more easily with the English, who would do almost anything to gain that end . . . .

(Margry, *MetD*)

From Governor Callière to the French Court,
October 16, 1700

In the spring, I will send sieur de Lamothe with sieur de Tonti to build a fort at Detroit. My plan is to send them to take possession of this post on the shores of Lake Huron by way of the Ottawa River, thereby avoiding the passage of Niagara in order not to give offense to the Iroquois. In the meantime I will take measures to improve communication by way of Lake Ontario.

In a letter written from Quebec, October 18, 1700 (addressee unknown), Cadillac outlines his plan for the new post in several major points:

1. The expedition is to be composed of 100 men, half soldiers, half Canadians, and is to be quickly undertaken to forestall the English. These forces will be enough for the first year, necessary for the fortification of the post and to provide adequate subsistance.
2. In the following year, after the founding, twenty or thirty families with their livestock and other necessities should be brought.
3. Two hundred young men who are skilled in various trades should be sent to the post.
4. Missionaries must be established at the post from the different orders. They should be responsible for teaching Indians French, for that is the only "way to civilize, humanize, and to insinuate into their hearts and souls the law of religion and the law of the King."
5. In the third or fourth year, nuns of the Ursuline Order or other sisters should come to the post.
6. It is important that a hospital be established for the Indians, as there is no better way to "gain their friendship than to care for them when they are ill or hurt."
7. The soldiers and the Canadians should be allowed to marry the Indian maidens who "always prefer to marry a Frenchman than some Indian."
8. These intermarriages "will cement the friendship of these nations, as the alliances of Romans continued the peace with the Sabines through the mediation of the maidens that the former had carried off from the latter."

It will be found that the execution of this plan will not only extend the glory of His Majesty with brilliance, but also that of the Lord, since by these means His worship and His religion will be founded in the middle of the people, and the awful sacrifice that they offer to Baal will be completely abolished.

(Margry, *MetD*)

1700
Cadillac returns to Quebec.

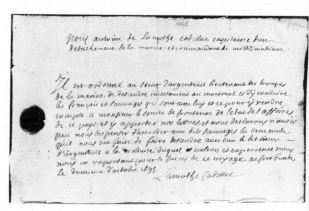

21. Travel Orders of sieur d'Argenteuil, signed by Cadillac, 1695.

"We, Antoine de Lamothe Cadillac, captain of a detachment in the Marine and commandant of the Mackinac militia.

"It is ordered that sieur d'Argenteuil, lieutenant of the troops of the Marine, go at once down to Montreal and conduct there the French and Savages who will go with him; and that he give there a record to Monsieur the Count de Frontenac on the state of affairs in this country; and that he carry there our letters; and we declare that we cannot refuse to grant to these Savages their request that said sieur d'Argenteuil go with them, he (who demonstrated) carefulness, valor, and experience on the journey he made to Fort Buade."

(signed) Lamothe Cadillac
(Document in the Burton Historical Collection)

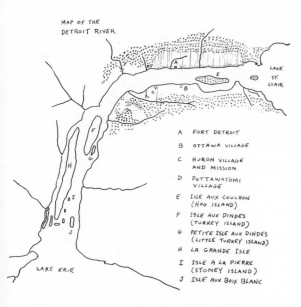

MAP OF THE
DETROIT RIVER

LAKE
ST.
CLAIR

LAKE ERIE

A FORT DETROIT
B OTTAWA VILLAGE
C HURON VILLAGE
   AND MISSION
D POTTAWATOMI
   VILLAGE
E ISLE AUX COUCHON
   (HOG ISLAND)
F ISLE AUX DINDES
   (TURKEY ISLAND)
G PETITE ISLE AUX DINDES
   (LITTLE TURKEY ISLAND)
H LA GRANDE ISLE
I ISLE A LA PIERRE
   (STONEY ISLAND)
J ISLE AUX BOIX BLANC

22. Sketch map of the straits, adapted from a 1749 map. The now-disappeared Savoyard River curves behind Fort Detroit (A)

1701

May 8—Cadillac leaves Quebec on the first leg of his voyage to found the new colony.

May 12—Cadillac arrives in Montreal to outfit his expedition.

The Jesuit missionary view of the results of intermarriage is different from those of Cadillac.

The Jesuits had been living in close contact with the Indian for many years. They had no illusions about him, and knew from accurate first hand knowledge that he could never become a Frenchman. What often happened when the two races lived together in too close contact was that the Frenchmen became Indians. The Jesuits gradually arrived at the conviction that the salvation of the Indian lay not in the fusion of the two races, but in a very definite segregation of the Indians from the French. In the pursuit of this policy they, of course, drew down upon themselves the charge of wanting to keep the Indian under their control for the glory, and even the enrichment, of the Society.

(Paré, *Church*)

Did the plan for encouraging Frenchmen to marry Indian maidens eventually prove successful? No, says Father Denissen in a letter to Clarence Burton written November 9, 1896, for,

Cadillac might have wished that the men of his party marry Indian women, but Peter Roy[who came to Detroit at the time of the founding] is about the only one who did so. Those vigorous pioneers did not shape their love affairs on the utilitarian plan. The young men grew lonesome in this wilderness, and their thoughts would wander back to the girls they left behind them. Permission was readily granted to any one who wanted to return to Lower Canada to secure a bride. Accordingly, as these treasures were imported to Detroit, the place grew more civilized and the inhabitants felt more at home and contented. The French of Detroit and vicinity never intermarried with the Indians to any great extent; there have been a few exceptional cases, but such marriages were rare, and, because so rare, they were all the more noticed.

[*It would be callous to exclude Fr. Denissen's 19th-century panegyric to the French mother, with which he concludes his remarks on the subject.*]
No bride suits the French heart as well as the frank, modest, polite, charming French maiden, who has the desireable faculty to grace her home as a queen and bring happiness to her surroundings . . . . The French home, with its contentedness, made the maintenance of Fort Pontchartrain at Detroit feasible. Detroit owes much to the French mothers of the eighteenth century.

The Algonquins knew the region later occupied by the voyageurs of France as Yon-do-ti-ga, a name still reverently preserved as the designation of Detroit's most exclusive men's club. Yon-do-ti-ga is translated into English, "A Great Village." So the Algonquins saw the region's destiny from afar.

(Stark, *City*)

Extract of a letter from Governor Callière to the Minister of Marines, October 4, 1701.

I already had the honor to mention to you, my lord, in my letter of August 6, that I had dispatched, on the 4th of June, the sieurs Lamothe, de Tonti, Dugué, and Charconacle . . . .

(Margry, MetD)

Extract from letter of Governor Callière, October 4, 1701.

Srs. de Lamothe and de Tonti, captains, Dugué and Charconacle, lieutenants on half-pay, departed the beginning of last June with 100 men, soldiers, and voyageurs, in 25 canoes loaded with provisions, merchandise, arms and tools, in order to build the settlement of the straits . . . .

The Recollects Father who was to serve as chaplain of the post was perhaps the Father Constantin Delhalle who died in Detroit. His first stay in Detroit must have been of very short duration for a baptismal record shows him officiating near Quebec between November 15, 1701 and June 5, 1702.

(Paré, Church)

Cadillac's route: from Montreal, up the Ottawa River, across to Lake Nipissing, through that lake and down the French and Pickerel Rivers, to Georgian Bay and across to Lake Huron, skirting the eastern shore, to Lake St. Clair through the Detroit River, to Grosse Ile.

The great canoes glided silently by the densely wooded islands where Lake St. Clair narrows into the beautiful straits. Cadillac looked about him and was pleased. He studied the lay of the land on both sides of the river, looking for the best site for his fort. Down river as far as Grosse Ile they went and there they spent the night—an encampment for which all loyal Grosse Ilers ever since have been incontinently proud, since it permitted them to say that Cadillac landed there before he landed at Detroit.

(Stark, City)

In the morning they came back up the stream, hugging the shore. Cadillac noted that the narrowest part of the river was faced on either side by a bluff about 40 feet high. This presented a dilemma: on which side to plant the fortified town that was to guard this strait; which side offered the best defensive possibilities. Observing the north side of the river, he saw that the bluff ended abruptly at its western end in a round-topped hill and around the foot of this hill poured the waters of a small river. The hill stood near the present foot of First Street and the small river, later known as the Savoyard, emptied into the Detroit River, near the present line of Third Street. Above its mouth, the Savoyard ran for some distance parallel to the Detroit River following a course that would approximate Larned and Congress streets. To the east of Woodward Avenue, its course turned abruptly north, crossing the site of the present Wayne County Building. The parallel course of the two rivers created a narrow peninsula of high ground, fairly level at the top and heavily timbered.

(Stark, City)   57

The Annals of Cadillac

June 4-5—Cadillac departs Montreal with 25 canoes, bringing his son Antoine (b. 4-26-92) with him. With 50 soldiers, 50 voyageurs and settlers, and about 100 friendly Indians, he brings his second in command de Tonti, two lieutenants, the Jesuit Father François Vaillant de Gueslis and Father Bernard Constantin Delhalle of the Recollects.

July 23—The expedition arrives on Grosse Ile after traveling approximately 600 miles with 30 portages.

July 24—Cadillac and his company leave Grosse Ile and return back upstream to the narrowest point in the river. He claims the land in the name of the King and begins to build Fort Pontchartrain, Ville de Troit.

The canoes landed near where Veteran's Memorial Building now stands . . . . Between the Detroit River and the Savoyard was a curving and rather flat topped hill; this is where Cadillac built the new fort.

North of the Savoyard River, where the large buildings of downtown Detroit now stand, lay the forest which stretched on toward the Straits of Mackinac. West of the camp the land dipped, just as it does today, to where Savoyard emptied into the Detroit River, and beyond lay a marshy strip of land which has since been filled in and forms the railroad yard along the river [i.e., now the Renaissance Center].

South of the camp flowed the River, less than a mile wide here. To the east of the camp could be seen Belle Isle. The log palisade was erected and named in honor of Count Pontchartrain. First called Ville de Troit, Village of the Straits, the ville was soon dropped.

From the records that have come down to us we can locate it generally as follows:

As one walked up from the river, whose shore then ran along where Atwater Street now is, he came to the wall of the settlement. The wall enclosed an area from about Woodbridge Street on the south to about Larned Street on the north, and from Griswold Street on the east to Wayne Street on the west.

(Lewis, *Detroit*)

Extract from a letter written by Gov. Callière, October 4, 1701.
Le sieur de Charconacle has returned with five men from Détroit carrying letters from sieurs Lamothe and de Tonti. The former tells us that he arrived with his entire company in good health on the 24th of July at the mouth of this river and that after investigating the area for the best location, he has built a fort composed of four bastions of oak piles fifteen feet long, embedded in the ground some three feet. Each curtain wall is thirty fathoms long. He has positioned his fort three leagues from Lake Erie and two from Lake Sainte Claire at the narrowest part of the river, west south-west. He first built a warehouse to store his goods and has begun work on the necessary dwellings, still in progress. He must keep almost everybody working to be done by winter.

(Margry, *MetD*)

Inside the stockade were the little oak buildings of the settlement . . . Ste. Anne's church, the warehouse where the furs were stored, and the log houses of the soldiers and settlers. All the buildings were one story high . . . made of logs set upright in the ground, but Ste. Anne's Church and the warehouse might have been built with logs lying on their side. The roofs were made from bark and thatched with straw or grass. The streets of the village ran east and west or north and south, and except for Ste. Anne were about ten feet wide. Ste. Anne Street, which was the main street, was about twenty feet wide. It ran about where Jefferson Avenue now is.

(freely taken from Lewis, *Detroit*)

By September 1, the site of the first settlement was all enclosed. It had an area less than 37 acres and during the next century of its existence, it expanded to less than a square mile.

The original stockade boasted three massive gates of timber. One looked toward the west, another toward the east, and the third toward the big river. The Indians gathered from far and near to build their little village in the shadow of the white man's town. They were Ottawas, Hurons, Pottawatamies, Miamis and Wyandottes. Peace reigned in this first year of the white man's occupancy.

(Stark, *City*)

The little village enclosure prepared by Cadillac in 1701 for the protection of his colony, covered a square arpent of land. An arpent, the French measure of that time, was one hundred and ninety-two feet and nine inches, so that the original village was in the form of a square, each side of which was that distance in English feet.

(Burton, *Building*)

Writes Cadillac in 1702:
You will see appended the plan of Fort Pontchartrain which I have built at Detroit . . . . The walls are of good timber, white oak, which is as hard and heavy as iron. This fort is in no danger provided there are enough people here to defend it.

Its position is delightful and advantageous; it is at the narrowest part of the river, where no one can pass by day without being seen . . . .

(Margry, *MetD*)

From Cadillac to MM. Callière and Champigny, October 8, 1701.
The art of war is not the same as that of writing. Lacking the latter skill, I draw a portrait of a land worthy of a better pen than mine; but because you ordered me to provide a report, I do so by telling you that Detroit is literally only a channel or a river of moderate breadth, twenty-five leagues long, according to my estimate, running NNE and SSW 41 degrees, through which slowly flow and slip away in a moderate current the lively and crystalline waters of the lakes Superior, Michigan and Huron—which are so many seas of sweet water—into Lake Erie and Lake Ontario or Frontenac, and then finally mix with the waters of the St. Lawrence River to mingle with those of the ocean.

Its banks are so many broad meadows whose grass is kept forever green by the freshness of those lovely waters. These prairies are bordered with long, broad lanes of fruit trees which have never felt the careful hand of the vigilant gardener, and, thus, under the weight of their abundant fruit they give way, and bend their branches toward the fertile ground that produced them. It is in this fertile land that the ambitious vine, never having wept under the knife of the industrious vintner, spreads a thick roof of broad leaves and heavy grape clusters, topping the woods to which it clings, often suffocating it in this tight embrace.

59

23. The arrival of Mme. Cadillac and Mme. de Tonti (Anne Picoté de Belestre) at Fort Pontchartrain in 1702. Mural by Gari Melchers (1860-1932). (In the Detroit Public Library)

In these wide forest avenues gather hundreds of timid stags and nervous hinds, with the bounding roebuck picking up the apples and plums that pave the ground. Here the anxious turkey calls, and calls again, leading her large brood to eat the grapes. And here also are the tom turkeys filling their large and ravenous crops. Golden pheasants, quail, partridge, woodcock, and turtle dove abound in the woods and cover the fields that are mottled by the branches of lofty trees, making a lovely picture that soothes any feelings of melancholy loneliness of the solitude. The hand of the pitiless reaper has never mown here the succulent grasses that fatten the great and heavy herds.

There are ten varieties of trees, among which are walnut, red and white oak, ash, spruce or white wood, and cottonwood. They grow straight as arrows, without knots, almost without branches except at the top, and they are of prodigious size. From them the courageous eagle looks fixedly at the sun, while at his feet is sufficient to gratify his bold, armed claws. The fish are fed and bathed in the clear crystal waters; their great numbers make them no less delicious. Swans are in such profusion that they might be taken for the lily rushes in which they gather. The chattering goose, the duck, the teal, and the bustard are so numerous that I must use the expression of an Indian whom I asked, before coming here, if there was much feathered game. "There is so much," he said, "that they have to open a way in order for the canoes to pass."

Can one believe that such a place, where nature has given so much with such order, will not yield to the worker who caresses its fertile body all that is desired?

In a word, the climate is temperate; the air purified during the day is a gentle breeze at night; the sky is forever serene, spreading sweet and fresh influences that grant the gentle favor of tranquil sleep.

If the location is agreeable, it is none-the-less important, for it opens and closes on the passage to the most distant nations on the banks of the broad seas of sweet water. Only the enemies of truth could be enemies of this establishment, so necessary to augment the glory of the King, the progress of religion, and the destruction of the throne of Baal.

(Margry, *MetD*)

July 26—Feast day of Ste. Anne celebrated in her new chapel in Detroit by Fr. Delhalle. The chapel is built slightly west of Griswold Street on Jefferson Avenue, fronting on Ste. Anne Street.

Tradition is that St. Anne's chapel was completed in two days, in time to celebrate her Feast day on July 26. Probably a shelter was erected but not a regular chapel. The term "Parish of St. Anne" appears in the registers for the first time July 17, 1722.

A church and a dwelling were built for the chaplain, Fr. Delhalle, where we do not know. The succeeding parish buildings as well as the cemetery were always at the southeastern corner of the enclosure, corresponding roughly to the center of Jefferson Avenue between Griswold and Shelby.

(Paré, *Church*)

In addition to being commandant, Cadillac has exclusive trading rights at the new post.

On August 31 Cadillac writes to Pontchartrain that,
    1) the fort will stand against any English or Iroquois advances;

2) he needs more soldiers;

3) Fr. Vaillant is working at cross-purposes to him;

4) some missionaries and their support should be sent as necessary to the establishment of the post;

5) he needs more boats for the transport of produce to Montreal.

Pontchartrain replies, in part:

Act in such a manner that the Jesuits become your friends and do not hurt them . . . . His Majesty wants the missions around Detroit to be taken care of by the Jesuits.

(Margry, MetD)

Cadillac on the Indian Settlements, September 1702

At a good distance to the right of the fort there is a Huron village to which I have granted lands in the name of His Majesty. I myself have planted the boundary markers and marked where I want them to make their fort and village. By this move I have placed all tribes in the position of asking me for land and for permission to settle here. There is also, to the left of the fort, a village of Oppenago, that is to say, of Wolves, to whom I have also granted lands on the condition that they will surrender them to me, if I later need them, in return for lands farther away; the place where they are might serve for a township some day. Above this village, a half-league further up, there is a village containing four tribes of Ottawas to whom I have likewise granted land so that in the space of a league there are four forts and, excluding the garrison, around 400 men bearing arms along with their families.

(Toujas, Destin)

Approximately 6,000 Indians live in the vicinity of the fort in the winter of 1701-2.

Extract of a letter from Fr. Enjalran to Cadillac, dated August 30, 1701.
I met Mme. de Lamothe who is quite set on coming to see you in Detroit. I should be very happy if the plan to send me in your direction allows me to accompany her. The great importance of the mission at the post you want to establish cannot be decided until steps have been taken for other missions, for the entire Upper Country needs reorganization . . . . I might yet see you before winter, and I would be very happy to support you in your glorious undertaking . . . .

(Margry, MetD)

October 31—The Company of the Colony of Canada is given exclusive trading rights in Montreal and Detroit in an act drawn up by Chambalon, notary of Quebec, on the orders of the Crown. Thus Cadillac loses his trade monopoly at the new fort.

1702
Spring—Mme. Cadillac arrives in Detroit with son Jacques and the wife of Alphonse de Tonti.

Mme. Cadillac travels via Lake Ontario, crossed at Niagara to Lake Erie, and then on to Detroit. Writes Cadillac,
Last year, my wife and Mme. Tonti set out on the 10th of September with our families to come and join us here. Their resolution in undertaking so long and laborious a journey seemed very extraordinary. It is certain that nothing astonished the Iroquois so greatly as when they saw them. You could not believe how many caresses they offered them, and particularly the Iroquois, who kissed their hands and wept for joy, saying that Frenchwomen had never been seen coming willingly to their country . . . .

Was Cadillac the First to Found Detroit?
There is one . . . subject of interest on which I desire to add a few answers

to the oft repeated question of "Who was the first white man at Detroit?" Not who were the first persons passing through the strait, but who first landed at Detroit with a determination to make that place his future home? This question would not have arisen except for statements in some of the earlier Michigan histories, which challenge that Pierre Roy and Joseph Parent were located at Detroit before Cadillac came. I believe the statement has no foundation in fact, and I will try to prove its untruth.

Cadillac asserts, in one of his early letters, that no one had ever visited this part of the country before. He certainly would not have made such a statement if two men were then living there, for he knew these men, as they were both members of his colony. Pierre Roy married an Indian woman. I take it for granted that he married her within a short time after first meeting her and that he brought her to the village as soon as they were married. Their first child was baptized on April 27, 1704, about three years after the village was founded.

Now this evidence is only circumstantial, of course, but it is sufficient to make one believe that unless Roy came with Cadillac, he did not come at all until the year 1702 or 1703. Detroit was a sort of neutral ground, not occupied by any Indians permanently, for it was above the lands of the Iroquois and below the lands occupied by the other Indian tribes with whom the Iroquois were then at war.

The other man who is supposed to have been here prior to Cadillac's time was Joseph Parent. Joseph Parent was the son of Pierre Parent, of Quebec, and was born at that place January 27, 1669. January 31, 1690, he married Madeleine Marette, at Beauport. He removed to Quebec where his first child, Joseph, was born, August 13, 1690. His second child, Marie Magdeleine, was born December 15, 1692; the third was Jean Baptiste, born 1694, '95, or '96; the fourth, Marguerite, born July 7, 1698; the fifth, Pierre, born about 1700; sixth, Marie Anne, born May 22, 1702; seventh, Gilbert, born December 3, 1703; eighth, Joseph Marie, born April 25, 1705. He then removed to Detroit where his ninth child was born, July 21, 1709.

If anything further was needed to show that he could not have lived in this country before the coming of Cadillac, we have a contract made by him on March 9, 1706, in which he agrees to go to Detroit, from Montreal, to work at his trade as master toolmaker and brewer, for three years.

I have thus shown conclusively, I think, that neither Roy nor Parent lived at or near the present location of Detroit in the year 1700, or before Cadillac came, but that Cadillac is, in fact, our first man.

Fr. Denissen wrote to Burton, Detroit, November 9, 1896, that
There is no account that any white man had his abode at the Detroit River previous to Cadillac. You proved satisfactorily that neither Peter Roy nor Joseph Parent could have been here before July of 1701. There is no ground for the belief that a Francis Peltier preceded Cadillac. It could not have been Francis Peltier, the son of Francis Peltier and Margaret Magdelene Morisseau, for he died in Lower Canada before 1698; his widow, Magdeline Thunay, dit Dufresne, married again at Montreal on the January 9, 1698, Peter Maillet. His son, John Francis Peltier, born at Sorel, Lower

Canada, August 15, 1691, came to Detroit with his stepfather's family about the year 1705-6, and married there March 25, 1718, Mary Louisa Robert.

Peter Roy married, probably in 1703, a Miami Indian, and took up his residence in the village of the Miamis, who had been induced by Cadillac to come and settle near Detroit.

(Burton, *Cadillac*)

December 10, 1702

M. de Lamothe received a letter dated July 18, 1702, from M. le chevalier de Callière who certified that the King had given the post of Detroit and Fort Frontenac to the Company of the Colony, and also wrote him to name this fort, Fort Pontchartrain.

On the 21st of July, M. de Lamothe left Fort Pontchartrain for Quebec where he signed a contract with the Company by which it agreed to provide subsistence for his family and to pay him 2,000 pounds per year. The contract was drawn up by Chambalon, notary of Quebec, and signed by M. de Callière, governor general, and Beauharnois, intendant. The same contract stipulates that the sieur de Tonti, captain, will also receive subsistance with his family and be paid 1303 pounds per year.

(Margry, *MetD*)

Cadillac writes to Pontchartrain, September 25, 1702:
It seems to me that they scarcely concern themselves here in Quebec with Detroit; the trade concession that the King has granted exclusively to the Company of the Colony has crippled Detroit because this Company has done nothing to advance it and no one can exist in a land where there is no commerce.

M. de Lamothe arrives at Detroit on the 6th of November, 1702, to find all the Indians away on the hunt.

Detroit's Early Population
When he left Detroit on July 21, 1702, Cadillac says twenty acres of land had been cleared, and the Hurons had 200 acres ready for cultivation. Now, six years later, in 1708, there were in all 353 acres, of which Cadillac had 157, all cleared by Indians and soldiers; the settlers had cleared 46 acres and the Hurons 150 acres.

In 1701, nearly 6,000 Indians of different tribes wintered at Detroit, "as every one knows" and what is more, Cadillac fed them all. How he managed this is a mystery, for "everyone knew" that the provisions had all been consumed on the way, and that Tonti had to go to Michilimackinac and to Fort Frontenac to buy "some refreshments." In 1704, Cadillac wrote to Pontchartrain that there were more than 2,000 Indians at Detroit. What became of the other four thousand is not said. By 1708, the number had dwindled to 1,200. Of the original 6,000 Indians, 400 were able to bear arms. Cadillac does not explain how, with his army of Indians, he kept

Summer—Cadillac first learns that his exclusive rights to all trading at Detroit have been given to the Company of the Colony.

July 21—Cadillac goes to Quebec to dispute the removal of the trade franchises from his hands; he is unsuccessful, but receives some compensation from the Company.

November 6—A frustrated Cadillac returns to his duties at Detroit.

Peace between the French and Iroquois permits opening of direct route: Montreal to Detroit—over lakes Ontario and Erie, across the Niagara, and finally up the Detroit River. Therefore a steady increase in Detroit population forces Cadillac to extend the village limits.

asking for 200 soldiers; or, rather, it is clear that most of the original soldiers deserted or went back to Montreal; in 1704, there were only fourteen soldiers left.

As for the white settlers, the numbers vary greatly. In 1706, Cadillac wrote that there were 216 persons at Detroit; and in the following year, Riverin, a friend of Cadillac wrote from Paris that there were 270 persons, including twenty-five families. In 1708, the king writing to Vaudreuil and the two Raudots, said that there were 120 French houses *within* the fort; and a few months later, Cadillac asked that five or six hundred inhabitants and troops in proportion be sent to Detroit. All the above information originated in Detroit, but in this same year we have the testimony of an inspector, named [Clairambault] D'Aigremont, who tells a very different story. "The whole of the inhabitants of Detroit," writes D'Aigremont, "numbered sixty-three. They have taken land within the fort, and have built small houses of stakes plastered with mud and thatched with grass. Of these sixty-three inhabitants, only twenty-nine have taken land, for the other—except the officers, Rané, d'Argenteuil, and Figuier—are only at Detroit for trading purposes." And in a note, he added, "These twenty-nine ought not to be regarded as settlers, for they are married soldiers most of whom remain at Detroit perforce; they are still performing soldiers' duty and mount guard like the rest.

(Delanglez, "Cadillac")

Disagreements between Cadillac and the Jesuits over the moving of the Indians from the Great Lakes areas to Detroit, the trading of liquor for animal pelts, etc., reach the governor general in Quebec.

The following points are outlined, September 25, 1702, by Cadillac and Fr. Bouvart, Superior of the Jesuits of Canada, in an agreement made by Governor Callière:

1. The Jesuits and Cadillac will stop their complaining about each other.
2. The missionaries in Ottawa country will urge, rather than try to prevent, the Indians coming to settle in Detroit.
3. Fr. Marest of Michilimackinac will go to Detroit in the coming Spring to minister to the Indians there.
4. Fr. Garnier will also go to Detroit to minister to the Hurons.
5. The missionaries of the Ottawas' country will be under the orders of Cadillac who will act in behalf of the King. The right of appeal to the governor is reserved however.
6. Private quarrels between Cadillac and the missionaries shall be settled by the governor and not be directed to the Court.
7. All disputes between Cadillac and the missionaries shall be discussed on the spot; if settlement cannot be reached, the governor will provide binding arbitration.
8. This document will be communicated to all the missionaries of the Jesuits.
9. Cadillac will be responsible for abiding by the terms of this agreement.
10. Copies will remain with the governor general and with Fr. Bouvart.

A fire at the fort in 1703 destroys among other buildings, that of Ste. Anne, and with it the church records. A registry of births, deaths, and marriages from 1704 to 1744 of Ste. Anne's church contains some of the leaves from the first records with the following notice.

We, Antoine de LaMothe Cadillac, lord of the places of Danguet and Mount Desert, commander for the King at Fort Pontchartrain, certify that the present book contains thirteen sheets being the first registry of baptisms and interments . . . .

January 16, 1707
(signed) La Mothe Cadillac

Extract of letter from Cadillac to the governor, dated August 31, 1703.
You ask me to be friendly with the Jesuits and not to pain them. Having thought it well over, I have found but three ways of succeeding in that: the first is to let them do as they like; the second, to do everything they wish; the third, to say nothing about what they do . . . .

The charge of illicit trading has been refuted so often that it hardly seems worthwhile to refute it anew. The first direct accusation at this period is that of D'Auteuil, a hypochondriac who was against practically everybody in Canada. The Jesuits as tutors of the Indians had a concession at Sillery which had apparently not been ratified by the king. In a law suit which they won, D'Auteuil claims, these Fathers obtained from the Sovereign Council half the seignory of Duchesnay, one of their neighbors. Not only do they take real estate but movables also. For instance, they are engaged openly in trade in the Ottawa country, where under the pretext of supplying their personal needs, they made, last year, more than 16,000 livres not to speak of other trading operations.

Pontchartrain, unwilling to let this accusation pass, asked D'Auteuil for an explanation. He also wrote to Raudot, the new intendant, asking to investigate the matter. Some kind of an answer was sent by D'Auteuil in the following year. He was speaking, he said, of the trade in the Ottawa country,

> which is public and against which everybody grumbles. Since it has been forbidden to trade in the woods, the Jesuits' canoes have been used by merchants and voyageurs to go to Michilimackinac where they trade heavily. Each year one sees these canoes come back loaded with beaver pelts. Can we believe that others than these Fathers themselves are trading, when it is forbidden to everyone else?

D'Auteuil's only proof of his charge is another question, which Pontchartrain could not answer. The true explanation was given by Raudot.

> I have inquired, my Lord, as to what might have laid the Jesuit Fathers open to the suspicion of trading in beaver pelts, as they are accused of doing. What has given rise to the accusation is that they are obliged to make use of hired men to bring the canoes conveying their provisions as well as the other things they need for their mission. Notwithstand-

1703
Fire at Fort Pontchartrain destroys several buildings and records.

Cadillac claims that his lieutenant, de Tonti, and the Jesuit fathers of Mackinac are planning to start a rival trading post at St. Joseph (Port Huron).

Cadillac charges Company clerks with illegal trading and punishes them. The clerks bring countercharges which result in Cadillac being called to Quebec. Cadillac is acquitted of the charges brought against him by action of the Lt. General of Canada, Claude de Ramezay.

ing all the precautions taken, these hired men cannot be prevented from taking goods on their own account, which they trade in for their own profit, and as they take such goods in the canoes belonging to these Fathers, people will have it that it is they who carry on this trade.

The real question of course was whether the Jesuits themselves were trading for profit . . . . Vaudreuil and the two Raudots writing to the minister gave the following explanation.

The Jesuit Fathers, my Lord, never did carry on any trade in the Ottawa country and they must assuredly be exempt from such a suspicion; but the men who bring their provisions to the mission do trade. When the Jesuit Fathers told you that what had given rise to the rumor was that the men called Desruisseaux and Des Pins, unknown to them, brought merchandise, they should have said that it was with their permission; for the merchandise which they allow those who bring them needed supplies is a sort of payment for the canoes and their wages during the whole voyage. From the time of Messrs. Frontenac, Denonville and Callière, such has always been the custom here; those who bring the provisions for the missionaries, Jesuits and others, have always taken enough merchandise to pay for their voyage. We must observe here that what the king gives for these missions is not even sufficient for the keep of the missionaries, and they could never stand the expense if they had to pay the men, for there is not a canoe which does not cost them one hundred pistoles to bring to the mission.

This joint letter then goes on to explain the case of the two men mentioned by the Jesuits. It was not clear whether all beaver pelts had been acquired during the voyage. Des Pins had been paid for these pelts in letters of exchange, and it would ruin the merchants if these letters were protested; moreover, Des Pins had thought that what he did was permitted. As for Desruisseaux, there is no record of his having brought any pelts to Quebec. "Those who carried the provisions for the Priests of the Foreign Missions may have done the same as Des Pins and Desruisseaux, but they did not bring any beaver pelts, for their canoe capsized at Sault St. Louis; they lost everything and one man was drowned."

In the two following years, the king wrote that the carrying of merchandise to the missionaries, over and above their needs, must stop, but he made no suggestion as to how the voyage of the carriers was to be financed. Finally, [Clairambault] D'Aigremont, in his report of 1708, wrote that a large quantity of goods was being taken to Michilimackinac by the canoes bringing the provisions to the missionaries; the Jesuits had no share in the trading, for the merchandise belonged to the canoemen and this was done with the approval and under the authority of the governor general.

(Delanglez, "Cadillac")

1704

Daughter Marie-Thérèse is born to the Cadillacs: first child born in Detroit.

February 2—Marie-Thérèse baptized.

Embroiled in trade and political squabbles, charges of plots and counter-plots, Cadillac is again forced to answer charges. He is acquitted but ordered not to return to Detroit. An appeal to Pontchartrain results in full exoneration.

June 17—The Crown repeats its intention to the governor general of wanting to maintain Detroit, while Cadillac reports to the Ministry on his conflict with Vaudreuil and Beauharnais.

July 1—Cadillac reports his arguments with the Jesuit missionaries to Raudot.

1705

September 28—Company of the Colony is forced to turn over its trading franchises in Detroit to Cadillac; he holds them for the next five years.

The Canadian authorities write on October 18, 1705, that "it was necessary to submit to whatever sieur de Lamothe wished," in order to avoid further trouble.

First Deeding of Land in Detroit

As early as 1704 the French Government authorized [Cadillac] to deed lands to the people, but it was not until 1707 that he knew that he was permitted to do so. At that date all, or nearly all, of the lots within the village were occupied with houses and a long tier of garden lots on the easterly side of the present Randolph street was used by the soldiers in the garrison. A good many farms along the line of the river, both above and below the post, were also occupied and cultivated by the French people.

Cadillac gave deeds of all these lands and lots to persons to whom he sold them. None of them was actually given away. They were sold upon conditions contained in the conveyance. These conditions were not all alike but were all of similar import. The deed to Michel Campau of a site of 53 feet on St. Antoine Street by 17 feet on Ste. Anne Street contained the provision that Campau should pay five livres and six denier annual rent and should pay the further sum of ten livres for the privilege of trading. This would make his annual tax about three dollars and ten cents. This tax was to be paid in skins, or in silver when there was coined money in the village. A livre was about twenty-five cents of our money; a denier was a small coin of different values at different times. At this time it was probably less than a sou or cent.

If the land owner wished to sell his lot he must obtain permission from the commandant who had the first privilege of buying, and if the sale was permitted, the seller had to pay a fine upon alienation. This fine was about one fourth of the value of the property. If it was paid promptly he was usually allowed to pay one-eighth of the entire purchase price.

There were some trades that could not be carried on without permission of the commandant, such as blacksmith, edge toolmaker, locksmith, armorer and brewer of beer. In order to obtain permission to engage in these trades a license had to be obtained from the commandant and a fee had to be paid for the privilege.

In some conveyances there was a condition that the vendee should join others in setting up a May pole before the house of the Commandant on the first of May in each year. Exemption from this condition could be purchased each year upon payment of three livres in money or skins. If the grantee of a piece of land did not improve it, it reverted to the government.

The first conveyances were made by Cadillac in 1707 and putting all the deeds together we are able to draw a plan of the little village as it was at that time. The picket line had been set back so that the village was about 720 feet long, extending from the present Griswold Street to Wayne Street and about 250 feet wide, extending from the present Jefferson Avenue nearly to Larned Street. Some of the old lot lines of 1707 can still be determined. The principal street was Ste. Anne Street and the smaller and less important streets were named St. Louis, St. Joachim, St. Antoine and St. Francis. There was also a Recontre Street or alley, and in later years a Campau alley. With the exception of Ste. Anne Street, which was about 18 or 20 feet wide, the streets were very narrow, not over ten feet in width. In front of the church the street was about 40 feet wide.

1706

Continued friction among Cadillac, merchants of Montreal, and the Jesuits. de Tonti removed from post on Cadillac's request. Sieur de Bourgmont replaces de Tonti for short period, January 29 to August of same year.

June 9—Order signed for Dauphin de la Forest to serve with Cadillac at Detroit.

Hurons, Ottawas, and Miamis camps at Detroit in sporadic fighting.

June 20—Cadillac in Quebec is ordered by Vaudreuil to return to Detroit to maintain peace among the Indians, not to trade outside the fort, and not to allow intermarriage with the Indians.

1707

November—Pontchartrain sends François Clairambault d'Aigremont to Detroit to investigate complaints that have reached him.

Cadillac made about 150 grants of land in the years 1707 and 1708. Of those that have been found there were sixty-eight deeds of village lots, thirty-one farms and thirteen gardens. There were a number of lots in the village that Cadillac retained for his own use. He owned the church, the warehouse, the wind mill and several other places. A description of one of his buildings will show the nature of them all:

> A house of stakes in earth 33 1/2 feet long by 19 feet wide and 8 feet high, half of planks above, with joints in a good ridge and the rest of stakes, and below half of beams with square joints, half mortised and the other part of split stakes . . . .

(Burton, *Building*)

1708

The second church of Ste. Anne is built.

The Church of Ste. Anne

The growing importance of Detroit justified a more fitting house of worship than the rude structure which had hitherto served that purpose, and in 1708 Cadillac began the construction of the first building in the settlement that deserved to be called a church. As usual he complained to the Court about the expense it caused him, and attempted to saddle its cost on the King. The answer to his petition gave him little comfort.

> However, as His Majesty has decided that he will bear no expense on account of that settlement, it will be very necessary that you should in future undertake those which are indispensably necessary such as the maintenance of the almoner, that of the surgeon and of the medicines. It is not right that His Majesty should defray expenses at a place which is not to yield him any return.

> The building of the fort, and that of the church are in the same category. It can be nobody but him who has the right to receive the profits of the country, who should be bound to do this building; and that must serve you as a rule in all that may concern this country in the future. You possess undoubtedly, the patronage of the church you are having built.

Fortunately, we have a brief description of the first real church in Detroit, and of its contents. When Cadillac learned that he had been transferred to Louisiana, he proceeded to safeguard his property rights in Detroit. An inventory of his personal property was drawn up and signed by Father Deniau on August 25, 1711. No mention is made in the document of the almoner's residence, but the item referring to the church reads as follows.

> Also a building, used as a church, thirty-five feet long, twenty-four and a half feet wide, ten high; boarded entirely above, with oak joists in a good ridge, and below of beams with square joints with doors, window and shutters, and sash frames between of twenty squares each; the whole closing with a key. Also a heavy bell.

The inventory continues with a long itemized list of furnishings and accessories for divine worship, down to the last "6 hand towels, half worn." From it we might try to reconstruct the sanctuary of the primitive chapel. It boasts a green carpet, on which stands an altar "of French walnut-wood with steps . . . and a tabernacle closing with a key." Over the tabernacle is a turning box, draped with velveteen "with a fringe."

Usually it presents a "small crucifix of copper or brass" but on occasion it can be revolved to bring to the front "a monstrance of silver without a stand." On the altar stand large candlesticks of painted wood, to which are added on feast days "eight bunches of artificial flowers, old and worn" inserted presumably in "four pots of red wood." At one side stand "two small credence tables of French walnut-wood, closing with a small bolt," and behind the altar hangs "1 large picture of the blessed Virgin of gilded wood." Suspended from the ceiling to serve as sanctuary lamp is "1 lantern of tin."

From a census of Detroit drawn up in 1710 we learn another detail of the church erected in 1708. It is located within the palisade, and is constructed of logs "laid one on the other" as is the warehouse. These are the only buildings differing from the others; even the commandant's lodging is of the upright log type. The chapel, we are told, also serves as residence for the missionary.

The congregation that worships in this primitive log chapel is also revealed in the same document. Delorme, Langlois, Parent, Des Rochers, La Jeunesse, Malet, "are all married and have their wives and children at Detroit." St. Aubain, Lafleur, and De Lisle seem to be the only soldiers at the post, and their wives are with them. Vin Despagne is a widower, and Chesne and St. Onge are virtually that, for after their names comes the comment: "Their wives will not go to Detroit." In addition to those already noted there are seven married couples in the post, four men whose wives have not accompanied them, and twelve "bachelors." If we add an undetermined number of children, probably fifteen to twenty, and a group of Indian converts increasing slowly in number since 1707, the picture of the little congregation is fairly complete.

(Paré, *Church*)

On March 25 the Jesuits are quoted as reporting that
this officer [Cadillac] is audacious and aggressive; that he thinks his power unlimited; that he always acts without waiting for authority; and that he gives to understand that he is the master . . . .

Report by the governor and his intendant, November 13, 1708.
There are only 63 households at Detroit instead of the 120 that sieur de Lamothe has reported to you. As for the savages, there are around 150 cabins instead of the 1200 sieur de Lamothe has mentioned. Of the 63 householders, 29 are married soldiers and the others are voyageurs of this region who have established themselves here. They go out every year and have houses in the fort only for trading purposes. Sieur de Lamothe is Detroit's largest landowner, alone holding 157 arpents of improved land while all the others together have only 46 arpents. There are three cows, six or seven steers or calves and one horse; it would not be to sieur de Lamothe's advantage if there were more because he could not rent out his horse at ten livres a day if there were more animals.

(Toujas, *Destin*)

Clairambault completes his investigation and files a report highly critical of Cadillac's administration of the post.

1709

The Court orders the troops stationed in Detroit to return to Montreal.

1710

May 6—Cadillac is promoted to the governorship of Louisiana, which effectively removes him from the entanglement of quarrels and charges in Detroit. Dauphin de la Forest is appointed to replace Cadillac at Detroit, but his health forces him to leave the post after a short time.

September—Renaud Dubuisson arrives in Detroit to replace Cadillac.

November 3—Cadillac receives orders to report to Louisiana to take up his new duties, but he delays setting off.

1711

June—Cadillac visits Quebec.

November—Cadillac goes to France, leaving his family in Detroit, to which he may have returned one more

Cadillac's removal from Detroit obscures his property rights at the post.

1712

Cadillac interests Antoine Crozat, wealthy financier, in the commercial potential of Louisiana.

September 14—Crozat obtains a trade monopoly in Louisiana to run for fifteen years.

October 24—Cadillac enters into formal partnership with Crozat in Louisiana enterprise.

1713

January—Cadillac sails for Louisiana.

June—Cadillac arrives near Mobile with family aboard frigate.

From a letter, the intendant Raudot to Pontchartrain.

If M. de Lamothe had been a different man than he is, and if it were possible to deal with him there would have been no dispute on either side. He had an order from you, my Lord, to assume this post and from the outset whatever he requested and was refused led him to charge that no one wanted him to succeed and that it was opposition to the settlement that he had orders to build. Nothing stops him. What opinion or regard can one have for a man who complains of something that he states in one of his letters to have been freely agreed upon.

(Toujas, *Destin*)

Detroit After Cadillac's Departure

We do not know just what change was made in the status of Father Deniau, but from the entries in the register it is evident that he remained [in Detroit] four years longer. This later period of his ministry was apparently not a happy one. He seems to have been attached to Cadillac, and when the latter was removed in 1710, the lack of his strong hand was felt, and a great deal of disorder appears to have crept in. The high hopes of Cadillac had not materialized, the settlers eked out a bare existence, and the rotting palisade was a symbol of the fate come upon a once possible rival to Montreal. In discouragement and dejection the missionary, perhaps reflecting the sentiments of his people, penned the following passage, with which we end the first ten years of our history.

In fact, Sir, Detroit is all in commotion, both within and without; order and subordination, whether spiritual or civil no longer exist, nor respect for authority, political or ecclesiastical. M. [Renaud] Dubuisson has had the fort cut into halves, has turned Madame (Cadillac) out and also the Church, and, consequently me with the six chief families here, namely deLorme, Parent, Mallet, Roy, Robert and Campos. I have forgotten the surgeon, who is not less necessary than the interpreter. It seems, from the bearing this M. Dubuisson adopts toward us, that he is infallible, invulnerable, and invincible. I do not say more on the subject, for if I were to tell you all, and sketch the portrait of Detroit for you as it is, it is terrible, it would affright you. As for me, I no longer live there. I languish and suffer there beyond everything that could be imagined, seeing its desolation and being unable to get away from it. Yet God be praised for all things, since nothing happens to us in this life but by the will of adorable Providence, and for our sanctification, when we do not oppose its designs. (Father Deniau to Cadillac, August 24, 1711)

(Paré *Church*)

The inventory of Detroit, taken at the time of Cadillac's departure on August 15, 1711, mentioned a fort of eight bastions, some houses, a magazine, diverse merchandise and supplies, a mill, thirty horned animals and a horse, all belonging to Cadillac; 400 arpents of cultivated land—double the area reported in 1708—plus the rents and quit-rents owed by the titular holders of 143 concessions.

(Toujas, *Destin*)

Cadillac writes, August 14, 1712,
M. Crozat is not alone in his Louisiana venture. Following your wishes, I have enthralled him and his colleagues with the commercial value of that region; I have regaled him with stories of the immense riches of Louisiana, with its gold and silver mines.

The population of the Louisiana territory is composed of approximately fifty soldiers and 200 French colonists. Cadillac sets out to establish a line of posts reaching to Canada, to keep out the English, beginning with a brick fort on Dauphine Island, commanding the defenses of Mobile at the mouth of the Mobile River. He is once again at odds with the local functionaries and the Indians; the commissary officer complains that he is giving government food free to the poor.

As a result of the Peace of Utrecht, Cadillac loses rights to his property in Acadia.

September 17, 1714, Cadillac to the Ministry:
You know, my Lord, at what pains I have been to carry along with me such a large family; since Detroit is so far from France and my own country, I have spent almost everything I have in order to get there.

Writes Cadillac, January 31, 1716:
I have never opposed such establishments; I can say, after a fashion, that that is my talent. But I am right to oppose the means by which they are going about it because they are not practical. What use to give a body hands and feet but no head?

When the ship bringing L'Epinay [Lespinay] arrived in Mobile Bay in the spring of 1717, Cadillac went on board to pay his respects to the new governor. The same promptly gave orders that his predecessor was not to land again and was to be watched. Bienville already had command of the handful of troops still remaining. In spite of L'Epinay's orders, Cadillac must have returned to shore, for he embarked on another ship, the *Paon,* and arrived at La Rochelle "with his whole family," on September 1, 1717. He was out of America forever. His only contribution to the American development was the assumed name Cadillac, which a vast American industry had later made famous.

(Delanglez, "Last Years")

The official records of the Bastille explain that Cadillac is "suspected of having made speeches against the government and against the colonies; accused of having written memoranda contrary to the welfare of the State." It is most likely that Cadillac, well familiar with the conditions prevailing in Louisiana, spoke out against the plans of John Law to raise investment capital for the development of the territory. John Law, a financial genius as well as speculator and economic gambler, responsible for the rampant inflation suffered in France, organized the Louisiana Company (Company of the West) and was responsible for the "Mississippi Bubble" that burst in 1720 when the false prosperity fell to pieces. Law fled France the same year.

1714
April 10—Cadillac is determined to trade with Spain; Crozat, who wants to stimulate internal trade, is opposed.

May 10—Cadillac petitions ministry to be allowed to return to France with family.

1715
February—Cadillac and his son spend several months in Illinois country in search for silver, copper, iron, lead, and antimony deposits.

Cadillac visits France and returns in 1716.

1716
January 31—Cadillac opposes Crozat's plan to establish advanced trading posts while Mobile is still undeveloped.

February 8—Crozat demands the recall of Cadillac.

March 3—Recall of Cadillac initiated.

July 24—Cadillac, learning of his recall, informs the Court that his continued presence is necessary because only he knows the location of the Illinois mines.

October 28—de Lespinay is named to replace Cadillac, with M. de Bienville to act as governor in the interim.

Duel between Cadillac's son and Benoit de St. Clair, cousin of a clerk of Crozat.

1717
January 13—Crozat's trade concessions are revoked by the Marine Board.

March 9—M. de Lespinay succeeds Cadillac.

September—On arriving in Paris, Cadillac is placed under police surveillance.

September 27—Cadillac is arrested with his son and imprisoned in the Bastille.

1718
February 8—Cadillac and son are released from prison without being brought to trial.

Cadillac, and later his heirs, attempt to reclaim the lost property in Detroit.

24. The Cross of St. Louis awarded to Cadillac. Now in the collection of M. and Mme. Combes of St. Antonin-Noble-Val (France), that family tradition holds to be the Cross that belonged to Cadillac, inherited by Mme. Combes who claims descent from the Cadillac family.

By mid-year 1718, Cadillac had finally received payment of his past-due salary, but now

there was another matter still pending: the question of his property at Detroit. While still in Louisiana after the death of [Dauphin] de la Forest (1714), he had taken de Tonti to task about the disposition of property, but the latter was even more determined than de la Forest and wanted to go to France to defend himself there. The fight over this property was continued by Cadillac's heirs long after his death, until 1787 when the Massachusetts Assembly gave Cadillac's grand-daughter, Mme. Gregoire, that part of Mt. Desert which had not been sold. His heirs finally abandoned the concession in 1811, and thereafter are "lost to sight."

Cadillac's own interest in the Detroit property is manifested in the flood of memoirs and begging letters which he let loose upon the Council between 1718 and 1722. A full analysis of this mass of writing would be wearisome, since each succeeding memoir repeats its predecessors with slight variations, and with unsupported accusations against all and sundry. How completely he misrepresented conditions at Detroit can be seen from the marginal notations made by Vaudreuil and Begon. The latter had succeeded Raudot as intendant, and the Council sent Cadillac's memoirs to them both for comment and clarification. The marginal "answers" of the governor and the intendant are dated from Quebec November 4, 1721, three years after Cadillac's first memoir to the Council on this subject.

They begin by making it quite clear that Cadillac was not at all instrumental in making the peace with the Iroquois in 1700. Next they remark that when Detroit was founded in 1701, the king, not Cadillac, had paid for it. The clearing of the land was done partly at the king's expense and partly at the expense of the Company; and later extensions of the clearing did not cost Cadillac a cent, since this work was done by the soldiers whose pay he himself kept. As for the fort of Detroit, it had been greatly reduced at the time of the war with the Foxes, and Cadillac's house is now outside the fort.

In one of his memoirs Cadillac speaks of the "whole of Detroit" having been cleared, that is, from the discharge of Lake Huron to the entrance of Lake Erie; but all the land cultivated, including that of the French and of the Indians, comprises four and three-fourths leagues (about 13 miles), quite a difference from the 125 miles that comprise the "whole of Detroit." As for the concessions granted to his children, to which Cadillac refers, no clearing was made and no house was ever built on this land; yet one of the chief conditions for the validity of concessions was to have had a house built on the land within a year and a day, on penalty of forfeiting the land grant. Instead of the 276 Frenchmen whom Cadillac claimed to be at Detroit, in 1721, the only French inhabitants there at the time were Delorme, Desrochers, Aubin, and the widow Beauceron, each of whom had two arpents frontage on twenty arpents deep.

The different tribes which Cadillac named as settled near Detroit were simply clans of one tribe. Cadillac, the administrators of Canada go on to say, cannot claim any reward for having enticed these Indians to come to Detroit, for the presents which he gave them were sent by the king or by the Company. While he had the exclusive privilege of trade at Detroit, only two tribes came near the settlement: the Potawatomis and the Foxes . . . .

He did not incur any expense for the forts which the Indians themselves built, for the gates of these forts were made by a carpenter paid by the king, "and no house was built within these forts for the missionaries, as there have not been any missionaries in the village of the first settlement until now . . . ."

The two Recollects [missionaries] were paid by the king from 1706 to 1709 . . . . The surgeon and the armorer at the fort were also paid by the king until 1709, when Pontchartrain wrote that from then on Cadillac would have to defray these expenses. Beginning with 1709, the chaplain at the fort was paid partly by Cadillac and partly by the Company, but since Cadillac later reimbursed the Company for this expense, Vaudreuil and Begon admit that the furnishings now belong to him.

As for the salary which Cadillac paid to the interpreter, he has been sufficiently repaid by the profits of the trade which he carried on with the Indians, since all trade would have been impossible had there been nobody to serve as intermediary between himself and the Indians. He neither fed nor paid any of the officers who served under him; but merely allowed Laforest to bring to Detroit two canoes laden with merchandise, while the other officers were allowed to bring one canoe each.

(Delanglez, "Last Years")

The King's decision on Cadillac's claims is issued May 19, 1722:

Cadillac has claim to all land cleared by him, not to exceed forty arpents in depth.

In all these cleared lands he has exclusive rights of fishing and hunting, and ownership of buildings erected outside the fort.

He retains rights to lands he granted to inhabitants of Detroit.

He retains rights to all belongings and movable properties which are his in Detroit.

He is to be repaid for ammunition and other goods taken from his warehouse for the defense of Detroit in 1712.

Cadillac's Appointment, December 31, 1722
(translation from *Mich. Pioneer and Hist. Soc.* 34 [1905], 297ff.)

Mayor of Castelsarrasin,
Antoine de Lamothe Cadillac.

Louis, by the grace of God, King of France and Navarre, to all those who shall see these presents, greeting:

By the edict of August 1722, duly recorded, we have created and re-established the title for offices, of governors, lieutenants and mayors in all towns enclosed in our Kingdom, the offices of mayor, lieutenant mayors, assessors, aldermen, consuls, jurors, clerks, for the town hall and their ancient, alternate and triennial comptrollers and the offices of lawyers

Late in the year Cadillac settles his family in St. Nicolas-de-la-Grave.

1719
Governor of New France refuses petition that Cadillac's son be made commandant of Detroit.

Cadillac and youngest son, François, move to Paris while Mme. Cadillac remains in St. Nicolas-de-la-Grave.

1721
August 1—Cadillac, in Paris, authorizes wife power-of-attorney.

1722
June 25—Cadillac's property rights in Detroit restored, he then sells them to Jacques Baudry de Lamarche, a Canadian living in Paris.

August—Cadillac pays 21,000 pounds for appointment as governor and mayor of Castelsarrasin, for which position he is to receive 420 pounds for life.

But Cadillac does not immediately take up residence in Castelsarrasin.

25. Cadillac's home during his last years in Castelsarrasin. The old carriage entrance remains on the right.

26. A 19th-century painting of the Carmelite Chapel in Castelsarrasin where Cadillac was buried. In 1813, the building was converted into a prison.

1723

September 9—Cadillac is inducted as mayor of Castelsarrasin.

and solicitors and others of like nature, which offices were suppressed by the edicts of June and August 1717.

And it being necessary to provide for said offices, we make it known that, on account of the full and entire confidence we have in the person of our beloved and faithful Antoine de Lamothe Cadillac, knight of the military order of St. Louis, and in his judgment, competency, loyalty, prudence, capacity, experience, fidelity and affection to our service:

For these reasons and other considerations, we have given and granted to him, and do give and grant by these presents, the office of Mayor, for us, of the town of Castelsarrasin, district of Toulouse, created by said edict of August 1722, which office had not been provided for. To have and to hold said office, and henceforth to be exercised, enjoyed and used by the said de Lamothe on a yearly salary of 120 livres which shall be made a yearly charge upon the revenues and franchises of the said town of Castelsarrasin.

Together with all honors, authorities, prerogatives, exemptions, rank, sessions, rights, fruits, profits, revenues and emoluments, which have been enjoyed, or the right to enjoy the profits of such office in full as existed before the suppression ordered by the edict of August 1717.

And everything that took effect by the edicts of August 1722 and December 1708, as much as it pleases us, provided however that the said Lamothe is 25 years old, and then accomplishes an affidavit to be passed before the said notaries at Paris the 10th of September 1722 here attached, under the seal of our Chancellor, at a penalty of losing said office, annulling these presents.

We hereby give and mandate our well beloved Duke de Mainne, governor of our province de Languedoc, or the commandant of the said Province and be the good life, morals, age, Roman Catholic religion of said Lamothe known to them take and receive in this case the required and customary oath, and receive him and put him for us in possession and enjoyment of said office and make him enjoy and use the same together with the honors, prerogatives, privileges, exemptions, powers, functions, rank, sessions, emoluments, rights, profits, fruits and revenues aforesaid, fully, peaceably and conforming to said edict and to obey him in all that pertains to said office.

Concerning said office, we request our beloved and faithful counselors, the ruling treasurers of France, in general of our finances in Toulouse, that through them, under whose jurisdiction are collectors, paymasters and other accountants, they do pay and deliver account to the said de Lamothe, each year, upon the usual manner and terms, the salary and rights of said office, to begin from the first of October past, and to require from the said de Lamothe only once a certified copy of the receipt for the money of said office.

We wish said salary and rights to be allowed at the expense of the accounts of those who have made the payment through our beloved and faithful treasurers and whom we request to do such without difficulties, because this is our wish. For which reason we have attached our seal at the foot of these presents.

Made at Paris, December 31, 1722, and of our Reign the 8th, by the King.

Castelsarrasin
Burial Act

In the year one thousand seven hundred and thirty on October the sixteenth, was buried in the church of the Reverend Carmelite Fathers, M. Antoine Lamothe Cadillac, knight of the military order of St. Louis, former governor for the King of the Province of Louisiana, chief of the Superior Council of the said province, and former governor of this town of Castelsarrasin. He died about midnight, aged about seventy-three [74?] years. MM. François de Lamothe Cadillac, his son, and Jean-Pierre Descombels, who have signed with me, attended the funeral.

Albepar, priest, curate
François de Lamothe Cadillac
Descombels

Noted in the proceedings of June 16 and August 3, 1731, in the inventory of the effects of the house made by the widow, were four paintings: one with a gold frame being a portrait of Cadillac, and three others without frames showing Mme. Cadillac, the eldest son, and the eldest daughter.
What has become of the Cadillac portrait?
I regret being unable to furnish you a portrait of the late Antoine de Cadillac. I have caused researches to be made in museums and private collections but as yet without results . . . .
wrote the United States Consel at Marseilles *in 1874.*
Dr. Marois of Castel Sarasin . . . is still searching earnestly for an original portrait of Cadillac,
reported the Detroit Free Press *in 1877.*
Continued inquiries have failed to turn up the only authentic likeness of Cadillac known to have existed.

Henry D. Brown reporting on his visit to Castelsarrasin on June 15, 1961:
I met Eugene Redon, a little man who ran a rope and twine shop, who is our guide. He is an amateur archaeologist who had excavated the alleged Cadillac grave. We went to the one-time Carmelite monastery, taken over by the Government at the time of the Revolution [1791, when the property was nationalized]. The prospect shown in the picture of 1870 (now in the Territorial exhibit) has been changed; stores are in front of the building; one sees only the tower from the side and down an alley. The building is in various public uses, part of which is a garage.

1724
The King removed Cadillac from municipal office; Cadillac retains residency in Castelsarrasin however.

1729
February 6—The last known legal act by Cadillac was signed by him at Castelsarrasin this date.

1731
Mme. Cadillac and three of her children dispose of the Cadillac house furnishings.

27. Maquette for a proposed statue of Cadillac by the Italian-born, Detroit sculptor Carlo Romanelli (1872- ?). The facial features are entirely imaginary.

Cadillac's Skull?

Monsieur E. Redon of Castelsarrasin wrote Mrs. Henry Brown on August 18, 1962, concerning his attempt to locate the tomb of Cadillac.

The widow of Lamothe Cadillac was buried at the church of Saint Jean on June 19, 1746. There is no indication of the exact location, as is the case with her husband. Tradition only locates his burial place near the entrance of the Carmelite chapel. Therefore, I excavated at that spot. With the consent of the mayor, I undertook these researches at the end of 1960. The skull that I discovered may well be that of the Governor, and it is not too imprudent to so believe, but it is difficult to come to definitive conclusions. With my cousin, the canon Gayne, I have edited a report, a copy of which I sent to Mr. Brown along with some photos taken during the course of the excavations. I was assisted in my work by Captain Souquet, but it was I who discovered the skull. I have kept it in my possession . . . .

M. Léonce Meyson, sub-prefect of Castelsarrasin, presented the Detroit Historical Society with a copy of M. Redon's report on his excavations, here summarized.

The Tomb of Lamothe Cadillac: Has It Been Found?

In 1904, the Archaeological Society of Tarn-et-Garonne undertook research in the old church of the Carmelites of Castelsarrasin where Lamothe Cadillac, founder of the city of Detroit, was buried on October 16, 1730.

The burial register does not indicate the exact spot of the tomb. However, referring back to the tradition that places it near the door of the entrance to the church, the excavations were made at that location. No valuable information was obtained, however. The matter thus stood for more than fifty years. But recent repairs undertaken at Castelsarrasin once again made this matter the order of the day.

The old chapel, turned into a prison in 1813, has undergone many remodelings. Recently the city planned to lay a new cement paving over the old brick paving at the entrance to the church. The old paving was coming apart in several places at the right of the entrance, exposing a rubble floor made of imported fill. Human remains were scattered in this ground.

M. Alary, mayor of Castelsarrasin, brought this fact to the attention of M. E. Redon, member of the Archaeological Society of Tarn-et-Garonne, who, with the authorization of the mayor, decided to recommence the old excavations in the hope of rediscovering, perhaps, the long sought tomb. Aided by a worker from the construction company, he dug an area, reaching to the side wall, about 2.2 meters by 1.2 meters. The fill dirt showed clear evidence of having been excavated previously.

At a point .75 meters below the upper paving, an earlier, no doubt the original, paving appeared, level with the adjacent street. It was made of bricks laid on the ground without mortar. Where some of the brick paving was missing there was clear evidence that an area had been hollowed out, certainly to hold burials.

In continuing these researches, M. Redon was assisted by Captain Souquet of the 17th Batallion du génie aéroport, and by the helpful advice of M. J. Salus and M. M. Redon, teachers at the municipal school. The canon Gayne, president of the Archaeological Society of Tarn-et-Garonne, visited the site many times.

The excavation trench was made with due regard to the fact that the floor of the church had been raised at sometime in the past. Five strata were discerned: at the bottom, a layer of mixed earth with fragments of brick; .28 meters above was a layer of river sand .03 meters thick; then a layer of dumped earth .20 meters thick overlaid by a layer of crushed brick of .05 meters; and finally, at the top, .08 meters of earth in which had been found the scattered bone fragments. On this compact foundation the last paving of the church had been laid of mortared brick. Probably the new pavement was laid .75 meters above the old to counteract ground moisture, but also to insure a solid foundation made uncertain by the frequent renovation of the graves. There do not seem to have been any tombs dug into this upper layer except for the bone fragments at the surface.

The excavation proceeded cautiously, for indications appeared that a burial had been made there. Soon we uncovered a skull that seemed to have belonged to a man over sixty years of age. It was very carefully removed. At this point, the new year's festivities interrupted the dig. Although precautions had been taken, some unknown persons got into the old church, during the break in excavation, and did some clandestine digging which disturbed the very fragile remains of the lower part of the head and the upper part of the body. Some bones were later recovered, but the confusion caused by the clandestine shovels made any careful identification difficult. However, under this burial, at a depth of about .30 meters, in a blackish layer of soil, we found scattered bones belonging to some earlier tombs.

It is difficult on the basis of these new discoveries to arrive at a specific conclusion. It is possible that the grave of Lamothe Cadillac, one of the last which was made in the Carmelite church, still lies undiscovered. The Archaeological Society, and others as well, have tried hard to solve the mystery, but further research has not been undertaken at this same spot. It is probable that the grave of the governor had been covered with a funerary slab on which his name was engraved although it would have been removed when the building lost its religious use, and the tomb would have been considered too difficult to repair at a later date. It is not unwarranted to believe, however, that our illustrious compatriot was indeed buried here and that the skull we discovered is evidence of the presence of his body having been laid there.

28. Modern entrance to the old Carmelite chapel of Castelsarrasin, which today is the municipality's festival hall. Excavations for Cadillac's grave were undertaken here. (Photo from a Castelsarrasin brochure of 1965)

A Pioneer of New France

Henri Négrié

This is an abbreviated translation of the talk by Dr. Négrié before the Archaeological Society of Tarn-et-Garonne, published in the Society's Bulletin 99 (1974): 37-55. (Authorization to publish this version was given to the Detroit Historical Society by the author.)

Some years ago I presented a paper on Lamothe Cadillac which was published in one of the Society's bulletins. But my report, which was based on local sources, contained some gaps as well as some errors. In light of research undertaken in Paris in preparation for the exposition at St. Nicolas-de-la-Grave (November 29, 1974-January 31, 1975), I have been able to fill these gaps and to rectify the errors.

The photocopies of documents which come to us from Paris are from various sources: the Museum of the Navy, the National Library, the National Archives, the Archives of Overseas France (at the former Ministry of Colonies), the Library of the Arsenal (where the Archives of the Bastille are found), and the Historical Service of the Army (at the Chateau of Vincennes).

Let us return to the country where Antoine Laumet was born and lived his early years. His paternal and maternal families lived very close to each other. St. Nicolas, the home of his mother, was a very large village and agricultural center situated in the rich and pleasant Garonne Valley, in the northwest corner of Languedoc. Two leagues to the south was Caumont, the home of his father, where the family owned several farms called "Les Laumets," a modest village dominating the greenery of the Garonne plain, on the lower slopes of the Lomagne, at the northern borders of Gascony.

Both families were highly respectable: on the maternal side were merchants, artisans, husbandmen; his paternal ancestry showed a marked attraction for the magistracy. M. Toujas has painstakenly reconstructed the large household of Jean Laumet and his difficult life. Forced into debt, he involved his relatives in endless lawsuits which generated divisions and tenacious grudges, despite the fact that he enjoyed the patronage of the Abbot of Moissac who was the lord of the region.

What was to become of young Antoine in this atmosphere of judicial investigations and uncertainty of what tomorrow may bring? Sporting his adopted name, Lamothe Cadillac, he entered the army as a cadet in the regiment of Dauphine-Lorraine, and later, at the age of 29, was appointed lieutenant in the regiment of Clérambault, which was garrisoned at Paris. This existence did not please him; he wished to emulate the pioneers who had founded New France in Canada. Travelers who had returned from the New World recounted its recent history: Quebec founded in 1608 by Samuel de Champlain, Montreal founded in 1642 by Maisonneuve, and the wave of peasant families who had emigrated from Normandy, Perche, Poitou, and Saintonge to clear, to sow, and to reap in the new lands.

He must have heard of the growing number of English wedged between the coast and the mountains (the Alleghenies), who opposed France and her Indian allies, the Hurons, the Algonquins, and the Iroquois. After difficult beginnings, the French recovered under a new leader, the Count de Frontenac, a governor of the first order and an experienced soldier, who organized the defenses and lined the frontier with fortified posts to guard against the English. Named governor in 1672, Frontenac drafted a political organization for the country, and, despite the opposition of the trappers and the Jesuits, he gave full encouragement to explorers. In that year he sent Father Marquette and the merchant Joliet to the still unknown Mississippi basin. Ten years later, in 1682, Chevalier de La Salle reached the mouth of this great river and founded Louisiana.

In 1687 war was about to break out. After the revocation of the Edict of Mantes, William of Orange organized Europe against Louis XIV in the League of Augsburg. France sent reinforcements to the New World. Two regiments embarked at La Rochelle, the regiment of Clérambault, with Lamothe Cadillac, and the regiment of Carignan-Solières. The latter already enjoyed a great reputation, since it had distinguished itself in Sicily in the preceding years. But Philibert of Savoy, Prince of Carignan, no longer able to support this regiment sold it to the King. After exchanging its red uniform facings for the blue facings of the royal army, the regiment took the name of its new colonel and called itself Carignan-Solières. It would be the first foreign regiment to serve abroad, in America.

Upon his arrival in Canada, Cadillas was assigned to one of the companies of marines that were scattered around Quebec. Some months later he was sent to the garrison at Beaufort, where he met Marie-Thérèse Guyon whom he soon married. In the marriage contract he not only changed his age from almost thirty to twenty-six, but also gave his fabricated ancestry. This usurpation of social status no doubt did not constitute a denial of his own family in his eyes. Wishing to keep the noble status which he had taken, judging it essential to the furtherance of his career, he could not reverse his actions and retake his old name. In a sense, he was a prisoner of the personality he had assumed. Yet, the alias alone was not enough; he also adopted the coat of arms of the family of Esparbès de Lussau, from the Chateau of Lamothe at Bardigues. Thanks to a cousin and a friend, he obtained from Governor Denonville, who had succeeded Frontenac upon the latter's recall to France, a grant of land in Acadia.

In 1688 war broke out. Frontenac returned to Canada where the situation was made serious by the fact that Canadians numbered some 20,000, while there were nearly 500,000 English. The war involved Cadillac, who faced the forces of the English governor of Boston who was trying to seize Maine. During Cadillac's absence, the English ravaged his estate, "leaving him nothing worth 30 sous" he reported.

Back in France, at Rochefort, where he served as a naval guard, he was confirmed in his rank of lieutenant of marines and departed again for Canada. Frontenac said, "A capable, well-intentioned gentlemen, who knows how to please and to make himself useful, should not be allowed to be lost in the crowd." As a parenthetical comment, I may point out the meaning of this position of naval guard, indicated on his official service record. It was customary when one had a rank in the marines, to grant a rank in the fleet, but at a lower grade. Thus, since he was a lieutenant, Cadillac was qualified as a naval guard, that is to say a midshipman, which he would have remained if disgraced and if he had not been confirmed in his rank of lieutenant. Later, upon his appointment as captain, he received a commission of naval ensign.

Cadillac had previously taken the opportunity to outline to

Pontchartrain a project which he had developed—the creation of a lake flotilla to form a link among the forts on the straits which would provide communications and facilitate defense. He arrived in Quebec with letters from the minister in which the king approved in principle the plans which were to be submitted to the governor. Frontenac, fully in accord with these plans, gave Cadillac command of a flotilla with the mission of revising the maps of the entrance of the Gulf of Saint-Sauveur and of the river as far as Quebec. He granted him 15,000 pounds, in the name of the king, and two companions of his choice, Louis Joliet and the engineer Franquelin.

In the spring of 1695 Frontenac named him captain of marines, with the command of Turtle Island at Michilimackinac, a village situated at the narrowest point of the straits connecting Lake Huron and Lake Michigan, From here, for two years, he successfully resisted the Iroquois allies of the English while maintaining the friendship of the French allies.

Although Cadillac spoke of the post with great enthusiasm, the situation was not as idyllic as he pictured it, for he was in constant conflict with his officers, who sought his removal, and with the Jesuit missionaries. Frontenac, who knew him well and appreciated his merits, wrote Pontchartrain that Cadillac

> would have to send you a journal this year to relate all the persecutions he has been subjected to in the post where I have put him; nevertheless, he has done marvels in gaining considerable influence over the Indians, who both like and fear him.

On Frontenac's death in 1698, de Callière, the governor of Montreal, was appointed to his position. Cadillac now addressed to him his views on establishing a new post. "It is a question," he wrote,

> of assembling in a single post all the nations—that is, the Indian tribes, our allies, dispersed along the Great Lakes—who will form a considerable city and will bring the English and the Iroquois to reason, and who will be strong enough, with help from Montreal, to destroy both.

Cadillac also went to France to plead his case as well as to interest the minister in the implementation of his plan. His success with Pontchartrain is reflected in the latter's support. Despite Cadillac's suspicions that Quebec might try to scuttle his plans, they were adopted and he was designated as the man to execute them.

On July 24, 1701, Cadillac arrived at Detroit to begin his fort. The plan that has come down to us is not an original document, but a copy dating from 1753 that conforms to the first design. The Jesuits wanted to send several of their priests to serve the parish, but Cadillac preferred to have the Recollects come instead. This decision would create another source of conflict for him.

Yet, everything seemed to succeed for Cadillac. He sent for Mmes. Cadillac and de Tonti. He had great visions: the establishment of schools and a convent of Ursuline nuns to educate girls, the founding of a hospital, and the marriage of soldiers to Indian women. He conceived of forming auxiliary troops composed solely of natives, to be put on the same footing as the marines, thus mitigating the serious numerical superiority of the English.

Henri Négrié

29. St. Nicolas-de-la-Grave Church.
Watercolor by William A. Bostick.

    Versailles was astir over these proposals, and his plans made progress. But his proposal to impose a head tax, in order to ease a shortage of money, was rejected by Pontchartrain on the basis that the king alone could levy taxes on his subjects.

    Several incidents aroused Cadillac's animosity toward the Jesuits. Father Le Vailland, who tried to approach the fort and its allies, the Hurons, was politely turned back. The priests, who were already upset by Cadillac's treatment of the Miami Indians, lodged a formal protest at Versailles. When questioned by Pontchartrain, Cadillac replied that he treated the Miamis with severity because they had massacred some Frenchmen. The minister, in turn, addressing himself to the Jesuits, replied that if the fathers wanted access to Cadillac's domain, they must address themselves directly to him and respect his authority. At the same time he advised Cadillac not to aggravate matters nor to create new difficulties with the Jesuits, who enjoyed broad influence.

Complaints were increasing on all sides in the entourage of the governor. People derided Cadillac, declared that he had delusions of grandeur, and mockingly called his new city the Paris of America. He defended himself as best he could and did not hesitate to denounce to the minister any action of the governor, de Vaudreuil, that he considered wrong. Pontchartrain rebuked him severely and forbade him to judge his superior in such a manner. Finally, Versailles was won over by suspicions. An inquiry on the situation in Detroit was prescribed and an order given to de Vaudreuil

> to convoke an assembly of the leading inhabitants and to invite M. Cadillac; then to demand of each a written statement of his opinion so that it finally could be determined what had to be done with Detroit.

Certainly, the charge against Cadillac was serious, for he was arrested at Montreal on orders from the governor and the superintendant de Beauharnais, for extortion and for abuse of power. The inquiry that had been ordered turned out favorably for Cadillac. "You can see now," he wrote with undisguised satisfaction, "that everything which I have planned has had an auspicious beginning." His promotion in 1710 as governor of Louisiana can be seen as a desirable advancement.

Assuming command in Louisiana, Cadillac, as a good pupil of Frontenac, thought first of organizing the defenses of this immense region and of creating from south to north a string of fortified posts which would reach to Canada and bar English access. He constructed a fort on Ile Dauphine which commanded the mouth of the Mobile River, where the capital of the colony, which bore the same name, was located. But a serious blow to Cadillac came with the peace treaty signed by England and France. The Treaty of Utrecht in effect dispossessed France of the entrance to the Saint Lawrence and access to Canada. Acadia, Newfoundland, and the Hudson Bay territory fell into the hands of the English. As a consequence, the properties of Cadillac disappeared without any hope of return to him.

The governorship of Louisiana was no sinecure. The long letters addressed by Cadillac to Pontchartrain do not reflect the same optimism and ardor which animated him in Canada. He experienced difficulties with the neighboring Spanish encroachments because the limits of sovereignty had not been established. Careful surveillance had to be exercised over the Natchez, who had recently revolted and massacred some Frenchmen. And the grievances were numerous: long awaited assistance which did not arrive; pay for the troops was years in arrears. There were also personal concerns: the problems of raising a large family in a land where resources were uncertain; the excessive heat for six months of the year. Cadillac kept requesting repatriation for his family. His pen was in constant use and his letters were excessively long, despite the advice of the minister who asked him to be more concise. Another blow was the loss to Cadillac of his valuable protector Pontchartrain, who resigned in 1714. The year after the

30. Governor's House in Castelsarrasin where Cadillac died. Watercolor by William A. Bostick.

death of Louis XIV, Philip of Orleans, who had become regent, appealed to the Scot, John Law, to reform the finances of the kingdom.

But matters were fast coming to a head. On October 28, 1716, Cadillac received the order recalling him, and granting a pension. He embarked for France with his oldest son, who had a personality as fiery as that of his father. For the son had recently made speaking against his father the excuse for a duel. The rest of the family had probably already left Louisiana.

After a three month's journey, Cadillac was put under surveillance by the police in Paris and soon arrested and placed in the Bastille with his son. Both men are mentioned in the records of the Archives of the Bastille of being suspected of uttering careless words against the government and the welfare of the state. However, their imprisonment was relatively

83

brief—they were freed in less than six months on February 8, 1718. We must assume that justice was done Cadillac, his name cleared, because in 1723 he was permitted to purchase the office of governor of Castelsarrasin. At the same time he received his patent of nobility and the Cross of a Knight of Saint Louis. Far from disowning his family, he occupied himself with the very complex business matters which were tying up the paternal inheritance. Cadillac claimed he was the only surviving male of his generation.

But his dreams of fortune had vanished. Henceforth he lived a modest existence. The records show that his contemporaries were unanimous in praising the pleasant nature of his reports and his benevolence, which made a happy contrast with the harshness and officiousness of the administration.

His wife had given him thirteen children. Only three survived and they married into the most honorable families in the region. His son became mayor of Castelsarrasin and died there, as did his father. Although no direct descendants of Cadillac remain today, there are some Laumets and Péchaguts in the region. The name Guyon is still well known in the province of Quebec.

The following is the result of genealogical research in the Departmental Archives of Haute-Garonne and of Tarn-et-Garonne; transcriptions of the pertinent documents are now held by the Detroit Historical Museum.

Jean Laumet was born in Caumont, a community adjoining St. Nicolas, to a merchant whose first name was Arnaud, and to Jeanne Péchagut, daughter of a shopkeeper of St. Nicolas. When widowed, and left with two sons, Arnaud Laumet remarried Jeanne Tissane and died a short while after having made his will on September 15, 1643, in his house situated at *barry bas de Caumont*. He named as his sole inheritor his eldest son Jean, a student, and left to his second son Guillaume 4,000 pounds when he reached 25 years of age. The will of the grandfather of Laumet-Cadillac reveals the existence of a sizeable fortune which provided the necessary funds for higher studies. Jean Laumet evidently studied law at the University of Toulouse where he was awarded the title of doctor of law. He registered as a lawyer in the parliament and entered into marriage on August 19, 1646, with a woman whose maiden name was identical to that of his mother, Jeanne Péchagut, probably a relative, who lived in St. Nicholas. He does not seem to have left Caumont immediately, since he was the district judge of his native village in 1650 and 1651.

Jean Laumet's brother, Guillaume Laumet, opened a business in St. Nicolas, November, 1654, and married Jeanne Dubon, daughter of the district prosecuting attorney of the abbot of Moissac. At the same time he bought a house fronting on the public square in the *rue del Faure,* where the father-in-law of Jean Laumet also resided. He became a widower sometime before the resale of his house on December 23, 1685.

The Maternal Branch

Jeanne Péchagut, mother of the founder of Detroit, was the daughter of Antoine Péchagut, a middle-class citizen of St. Nicolas, and of Anne Gibrac, sister of François Gibrac, court secretary of the royal district court of Castelsarrasin. Widowed in 1636, Antoine Péchagut shared his lodgings with his daughter, Jeanne, and his son-in-law, Jean Laumet, who, after a brief stay at Castelsarrasin, had obtained in 1652 from the abbot of Moissac the office of deputy of the judge of St. Nicolas. His house was located in the *rue del Faure* behind the public square and backed on the *rue Poutou de Douan.* There was born Antoine Laumet, on March 5, 1658. Therefore, it is right that the *rue del Faure* had its name changed at the beginning of this century to *rue Lamothe-Cadillac.*

The Activities of Jean Laumet

The marriage in August, 1646, of Cadillac's parents, Jean Laumet and Jeanne Péchagut, consecrated the union of the two families who owed much to the protection of the abbots of Moissac. This benevolence did not come to an end, since Jean Laumet became, in September, 1652, deputy to the judge of St. Nicolas. The following year in the midst of the Fronde (a revolt against Mazarin during the minority of Louis XIV), he was named first counsel of a little village, which, taking into consideration the very difficult

Jean Laumet, Father of Antoine Laumet de Lamothe Cadillac and his Children
René Toujas

circumstances, was a mark of confidence. His nomination to judge of St. Nicolas in 1664 was the crowning point of his professional career. On September 11, 1653, Jean Laumet had the courtyard of the parish church paved and flagstones laid. Relieved of his counselor functions, he became *prior* in 1657 of the Chapel of the Penitents of St. Nicolas, a brotherhood partially restricted since the members were habitually recruited from among the notables of the parish.

In addition to his judicial or political obligations, Jean Laumet was a landowner. During the period of troubles and poverty caused by the Fronde, Jean Laumet was extremely active buying various properties in the area and increasing the domain of the Laumets situated in the plain of Caumont. He traded with the citizens of his native village and made seed available to a number of farmers who thus stood in his debt. But he also got into debt himself in exercising his counselor functions. Interminable lawsuits had drastic consequences for the Laumet family; ruin and discord followed it.

The Children of Laumet-Cadillac's Parents

Jean Laumet and Jeanne Péchagut had numerous children. Their oldest daughter, Cadillac's sister, Anne—born April 1, 1648 in St. Nicolas—was married September 20, 1665, to a citizen of St. Nicolas, Pierre de Lasserre. Three sons were born to her.

Examination of the parish registry of St. Nicolas reveals the baptismal records of the other children of Judge Laumet. The eldest son, François, was born in 1654. A philosophy student in 1671, he joined the king's guard around 1680. On June 26, 1684, he married in Toulouse one Louise d'Auriol de Peyrens, a member of a noble family in the environs of Castelnaudary.

A daughter Antoinette was baptized on December 4, 1653, but she must have died young for she was not mentioned in her father's will.

One of two sisters called Jeanne (we have the baptism record, however, of only one) was born on January 6, 1656.

On March 10, 1658, Antoine Laumet (Cadillac) was carried to the baptismal font by his maternal grandparents. No other document pertaining to the youth of Cadillac has been found.

On November 23, 1670, Jean was baptized, held by his godfather Jean Lanes, son-in-law of the judge. He was to die very young.

On April 27, 1673, Perrette Laumet was born; she married on June 21, 1695, Pierre Mauquié, soldier-at-arms living in the jurisdiction of Castéra-Bouzet.

The youngest girl of the family, Paule, was born on June 22, 1674. She cared for her father in his old age, while he in turn gave her certain rights on January 6, 1699, "so that she can deal and negotiate as a liberated person can." After the death of her father Paule Laumet married Marshall de Fossat-Plaignes, judge at the court of the Assistants of Montauban.

The elder of Cadillac's two sisters named Jeanne was married on May 23, 1670, in the neighboring parish church at Moutet, to the lawyer of parliament Jean Lanes, living in St. Sardos, a commune of the canton of

Verdun-sur-Garonne. This marriage greatly pleased Judge Laumet who asked the young couple to be the godparents of the son Jean born November 23, 1670, and of his youngest daughter Paule's baptism on June 24, 1674. Jean Lanes died around 1694.

The younger sister, Jeanne, married at Caumont, on April 13, 1688, a middleclass citizen Guillaume Cabirol, native of Causé (a canton of Beaumont-de-Lomagne), who died July 10, 1701. Their son was a lawyer in the parliament in 1717.

In an act of concession dated September 1, 1691, François explained that the money from the sale of property was necessary for him to go into the service of his Majesty. Jean Laumet mortgaged a piece of land in Caumont, on March 28, 1692, to pay for a mare with harness that he "leases to M. Laumet the younger who has to leave tomorrow for the service of the king in his armies." It is remarkable that the three sons of the judge of St. Nicolas, like many of their compatriots from Gascony— d'Artagnan the most notable—chose the career of arms in order to earn a living.

On his release from the Bastille, Cadillac drew up, with his brother-in-law and nephews, a general succession ruling that we know only from the extracts published by a local scholar, Edouard Forestié, in the *Bulletin of the Archeological Society of Tarn-et-Garonne* in 1907: "All the proper-

31. Town Hall and Square of St. Nicolas-de-la-Grave. Watercolor by William A. Bostick.

ties named and investments having belonged to his parents and to his older brother and abandoned by them are in litigation among the claimants on the rights of succession of the said deceased.'' He declared ''he was the sole male of the family'' and that he ''had the right to know the state and contents of the said succession.'' This included ''a dilapidated house at Caumont, meadows near Angeville, belongings at St. Nicolas, a run-down house situated on the public square in the said St. Nicolas, a field and a pigeoncote, etc., all estimated at 1800 pounds.'' France was undergoing then the inflationary effects of John Law's manipulations, but this evaluation appears excessive, judging by the modest sums that formerly belonged to Judge Laumet. On the other hand, the description of the inhabited buildings seems reasonable since the inheritance, weighted with mortgages, had been involved in litigation that forestalled division for twenty years. It is evident that no inheritor had enough interest to undertake the upkeep of the houses built in stucco in a situation so uncertain. At long last Cadillac became proprietor of all the family properties, after having indemnified his two younger sisters, Perrette and Paule.

The plan of the house at the end of the 18th century, preserved in the city hall of St. Nicolas, mentions that on this street there was a Péchagut building which is noted as being the birthplace of Cadillac.* The family of Cadillac, therefore, could not have preserved it. Finally, we know that during his lifetime Cadillac gave the use of the family home to his wife Marie-Thérèse de Guyon, who lived there and took care of the administrative duties. Cadillac probably turned over to her the administration of his property because he was more interested in the affairs which were taking place in Paris, if not at the Court, rather than in the circumscribed monetary speculations of a modest property owner in Gascony.

His descendants did not remain in St. Nicolas. The Laumet family has disappeared. Thus it was that the buildings, which had been acquired with such difficulty and which were laboriously preserved in the 18th century by men of limited means, passed through so many hands over the years. And these 18th-century notables owed their social positions and probably the success of their children to the protection of the lord of the region, the powerful abbot of Moissac. But was it not this type of patronage that was largely responsible for Cadillac's amazing career?

*For the evidence which indicates that the present house is the same dwelling in which Cadillac was born, see the chapter by Solan Weeks.

Cadillac and Marie-Thérèse de Guyon had thirteen children born between 1690 and 1710. Only two sons and a daughter—Joseph, François, and Marie-Thérèse—were alive when their father's estate was probated in 1731. Mme. Cadillac survived her husband, dying in 1746 in Castelsarrasin. The assumed name of Lamothe Cadillac was retained by the sons.

There is some conflict in the birth dates of Cadillac's children, and several remain shadow figures for lack of documents. The following list appears to be reasonably accurate.

Judith: Probably the oldest of the children, born 1689. She was articled to the Ursuline nuns November 12, 1711, to be a perpetual pensioner, her father paying 6,000 pounds for her support.

Joseph: The oldest son, born circa 1690. He is named in the records of Castelsarrasin.

Antoine: Born April 26, 1692, he came to Detroit with Cadillac in 1701; later entered the military.

Magdelene: Probably born at either Port Royal or Mt. Desert. Served as godmother at baptism in Detroit, 1706.

Jacques: Born March 16, 1695, in Quebec; came to Detroit with Mme. Cadillac in 1702.

Peter Denis: Born June 13, 1699, in Quebec, where he died July 4, 1700.

Marie Anne: Born June 7, 1700, in Quebec, where she died almost exactly a year later, June 9, 1701.

(   ): A "child" born and died in late 1702, in Detroit. Mentioned in a letter of Cadillac, its baptism record may have been destroyed in the fire at Ste. Anne.

Marie-Thérèse: Born or baptized February 2, 1704, in Detroit. She married in Castelsarrasin on February 16, 1729, François Hercule de Pouzargues. No children. Died February 1, 1753.

Jean Antoine: Baptized January 19, 1707, in Detroit; buried there April 9, 1709.

Marie Agathe: Born December 28, 1707, and baptized the next day in Detroit.

François: Born March 27, 1709 (1703?) and baptized the next day. He was married in Castelsarrasin, September 10, 1744, to Angelique Furgole, widow of Pierre Salvignac, and daughter of Jean Furgole. No children.

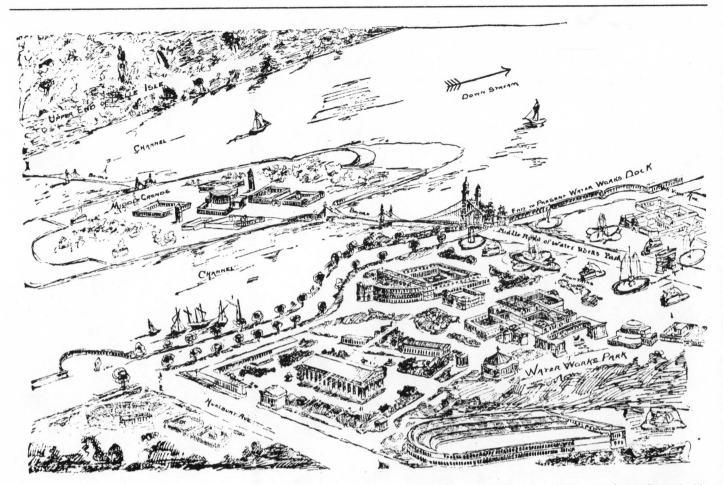

René Louis: Born March 17, 1710 and baptized the next day in Detroit. He died and was buried in Quebec October 7, 1714.

The oldest son of Cadillac, Joseph, married Marguerite de Gregoire; they had at least two children: Marie-Thérèse and Marguerite Anne. The baptismal record of Marie-Thérèse is preserved in Castelsarrasin.

In the year 1733 on the 29th of April, there was baptized in the Church of the Savior, Marie-Thérèse de Lamothe Cadillac, daughter of Joseph de Lamothe Cadillac and Margurerite de Gregoire his wife of this parish, born the 28th of this month, at 1 o'clock, p.m. Godfather, Guillaume Caunac, old guard of the King; Godmother, Marie-Thérèse de Guyon, widow of Antoine de Lamothe Cadillac, former governor of this town, who have signed this with me.

(signed) Marie-Thérèse de Guyon, widow of de Lamothe Cadillac
     Lamothe Cadillac
     Caunac de Louzargues, provost.

This granddaughter of Cadillac married Bartholomy de Gregoire, and had three children: Pierre, Nicolas, Maria.

The marriage certificate of Cadillac's son François and Angelique Furgole has survived. (Translation from the *Michigan Pioneer and Historical Society*, 34, 1905)

In the year 1744, September 10th, François Lamothe Cadillac, son of

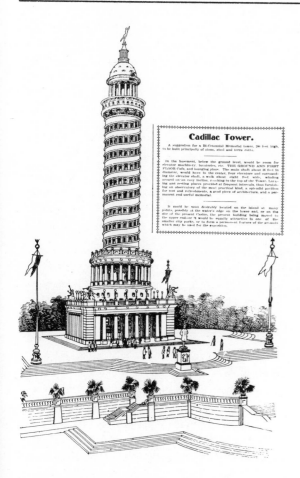

the late Antoine Lamothe Cadillac, Knight of the military order of St. Louis, heretofore Governor for the King in the province of Louisiana, Premier of the superior Council of the said Province, and ancient governor of this city, and Marie-Thérèse de Guyon, party of the first part; and Mlle. Angelique de Furgole, widow of Pierre Salvignac, citizen, and daughter of the late Jean Furgole, notary, and Mme. Marie Dane, party of the second part; after the publication of three marriage bans, duly made at our parish mass, on three consecutive Sundays or holidays, without any obstacle or opposition having appeared, and after the observation of other formalities, in such cases required, have been joined in wedlock, by us undersigned rector in the Church of the Savior of this city, of which both parties are parish members, and in the presence of François Louzarques, Bertrand Oarant, furrier, of Guillaume Magnes, merchant, Philippe Bóe, doctor, who signed with the said parties.

> (signed) Lamothe Cadillac
> Angelique de Furgole
> De Louzarques
> Magnes
> Oarant
> Boe
> Orades, rector.

32, 33, 34. Elaborate plans for reconstructing Detroit's waterfront to celebrate the bicentennial of the founding of the city were drawn up by the architect Louis Kamper in 1901. A ''Cadillac Tower'' and a ''Cadillac Memorial Column'' topped with a statue of the city's founder were to have been part of the new exposition complex. This elaborate plan was never realized. (Illustrations: Burton Historical Collection)

In 1904, a Marie Lasserre addressed herself to the acting mayor of Detroit as a descendant of Cadillac. Her name is not without interest, for Cadillac's eldest sister, Anne, married Pierre Lasserre; and the youngest of Cadillac's sisters, Paule, was presented for baptism by godparents named Lasserre.

St. Sardos, Tarn-et-Garonne
February 24, 1904

Mayor John Harper
(acting for Mayor Lodge)
Detroit, Michigan

Dear Mayor,

I have not received answers to any of the letters which I have written to you and which consisted of requests for help in my position as a descendant of the Chevalier Lamothe Cadillac, otherwise known as Antoine de Laumet, the glorious founder of your city. As I have already said, Mr. Mayor, I again make an appeal to the charity and to the generosity of the people of the Queen of the Lakes. The descendants of Antoine de Laumet, once in wealth, are now reduced to the blackest misery. Unfortunate and abandoned sufferers, they now turn to you, Mr. Mayor, in the hope that through the generosity of the people of your rich and prosperous city, thanks will be rendered for the providential safety they have enjoyed for so long a time . . . .

The revolution of '89 began the debacle our fortune suffered; two of our grand uncles died émigrés, their wealth being seized by the government!

Our eldest brother, adored by our family, died in 1870 defending St. Liege. I am alone in the world with my brother, always ill. The infirmities of age and miseries beset my life, and in my distress I turn to you, hoping that you can help a poor woman whose ancestor believed your city so rich and prosperous . . . .

The sentiment of veneration which has been preserved and the regard which you profess for Lamothe Cadillac have made me hope that you will lend a hand to us . . . .

I wish to tender to you, Mr. Mayor, and to the members of your city council, my regard and my respect.

(signed) Marie Lasserre

Henry D. Brown reported on his visit to France that on June 18, 1961, he went to:

St. Lys, met Counte Armand de Pouzarques, a great-great-great grandson of Cadillac, who is 92. He is deaf and can only respond to written messages. He was a rancher in USA for seven years, in the West; said he had never visited Detroit. Went into his house to see mementoes, some family pictures of the early 1800's, four oil portraits (not Cadillac or family). He read and spoke English well. Mme.

Dague had located him by her research, and also made possible the arrangements for filming folklore festival.

According to Négrié, "Today no direct descendants of Lamothe-Cadillac remain. But there are still some Laumets and Péchaguts in the region. And still the name of Guyon is well-known in the province of Quebec."

The Preservation of Cadillac's Birthplace

Solan Weeks

Ever since the day in 1904 when the Archaeological Society of Tarn-et-Garonne erected a marker on a small, single story brick structure just off the town square of St. Nicolas-de-la-Grave, France, proclaiming it as the birthplace of Antoine Laumet de Lamothe Cadillac, Detroiters have been concerned with the preservation of this tangible link with our city's founder.

St. Nicolas, a village in Cadillac's time, still remains a village. It is situated in southwestern France, due south of Paris, and close to the Spanish border. Nearby are the small city of Moissac with its splendid Romanesque church, the larger city of Montauban, and Castelsarrasin where Cadillac is buried. Over the years, numerous Detroiters have made the pilgrimage to St. Nicolas to visit this humble dwelling, and on several occasions plans were formulated to insure the preservation of the structure.

The first official journey was made in 1907 by Clarence Monroe Burton, historian for the city of Detroit. He described the house of Cadillac's birth and the pleasant village of St. Nicolas. In the 1920's, Burton proposed that the structure be purchased, taken apart, and transported to Detroit where it could be re-erected in a prominent location as a lasting monument to the city's founder. The plan failed to materialize.

In 1924, John Hubert Greusel visited St. Nicolas and later wrote a pamphlet on the mystery of Cadillac's lost grave. Milo M. Quaife traveled to St. Nicolas in September, 1955, with his wife and wrote of his experiences in the *Bulletin* of the Detroit Historical Society. He described the two-story wing on the Cadillac house which was later removed because there was no evidence that the original Cadillac house had been occupied above the main floor. He noted that the exterior of the building was unchanged from its appearance in 1904, while the "interior of the house, however, presents a dismal appearance."

As a part of the official commemoration of the 300th anniversary of the birth of Cadillac in March, 1958, Mayor Georges Doustin of St. Nicolas and Adrien Alary, mayor of Castelsarrasin, where Cadillac had served as governor and later died, were entertained in Detroit. On their departure for France, they extended invitations to the members of the civic committee for the Cadillac Tercentenary to visit France in July for their celebrations. This festive occasion on July 3-6, 1958, was to celebrate Cadillac's birthday as well as the 150th anniversary of the establishment of the local department which was created by Napoleon from a patchwork of provinces in southern France in 1808. Reuben Ryding, an honorary trustee of the Detroit Historical Society, his wife, and their companions, Mrs. Charles McCormick and her son Ronald of Tawas City, Michigan, attended this unique celebration. Walker Cisler, co-chairman of the Office of International Relations, was able to break away from his responsibilities as chairman of the Board of the Detroit Edison Company to attend the final day of celebration, Sunday, July 6.

The Detroit delegation had expected to be merely spectators, but they became guests of honor, representing Detroit and the United States of America. They were swept up in four days of receptions, luncheons, *vins d'honneur,* and dinners; of toasts, speeches, and responses. Within the memory of anyone they saw, they were the first American tourists who had

ever visited Castelsarrasin and St. Nicolas. The Office of the U. S. Information Service in Toulouse sent Robert Tricorre and Jacqueline Gelo as interpreters, and the USIS in Bordeaux sent its assistant director, Stanley Alpern, to assist the Detroiters during the celebration.

Following Reuben Ryding's visit to St. Nicolas, a Detroit Historical Society Committee was formed to explore steps which could be taken to give adequate recognition to Cadillac. Ryding chaired the committee, and at his suggestion, the committee recommended to the Society Board of Trustees the production of a sound-color motion picture on Cadillac's homeland.

Through the assistance of George Pierrot of the World Adventure series program, the services of photographer-lecturer Arthur Wilson and his partner Fred Keiffer of Chicago were enlisted. With Henry D. Brown, the former director of the Detroit Historical Department and coordinating Director of the Detroit Historical Society, they documented on film and paper the landmarks and sites associated with the city's founder. The mayor of St. Nicolas, Jean Lafougere, enabled the team to gain access to various structures and to block off local streets to eliminate modern traffic during the filming. The resulting film provided a sense of reality to Detroit's founder that had not existed before. Whereas nothing remains of the early

35. The birthplace of Cadillac on Avenue Lamothe Cadillac. View of the house still the property of the Bêche family, before restoration. The outline of the bricked-up door beneath the window (closest to the commemorative plaque) is just visible. The wall of the adjoining building shows the missing brickwork where an earlier second floor probably keyed into the wall.

95

French period in Detroit, Cadillac's homeland still displays the landscape and many buildings almost unchanged since the 18th century.

Henry Brown noted in his diary in October, 1961, that Cadillac's house was in

> a sad state of disrepair. The interior has obviously been changed several times. Restoration would take a good bit of historical archaeology. In the rear room, now unused except for storage, the big fireplace could well be of Cadillac's period.

A few pages later he wrote that the "present owners of the Cadillac house would ask a price of $25,000, an impossible sum for the building and land," which had prevented any local attempt to restore the structure.

Again in 1965 Brown re-opened the question of acquiring and preserving the Cadillac birthplace. He wrote Mayor Lafougere,

> If the building were restored, it should be of interest to many tourists . . . . if the building could be obtained for a reasonable price, it is possible that a potential donor or donors might be interested in its purchase and restoration.

In the years that followed many Detroiters made the pilgrimage to Cadillac's birthplace. When I became the Director of the Detroit Historical Museum in September, 1970, six months after the death of Henry Brown, I found a letter waiting for me from Émile Boutel, a resident of St. Nicolas who had met Brown during his trip to France in 1961, and who had continued to correspond with him. Boutel wished to continue his liaison with Detroit, and I assured him of my desire to do so, and I also inquired as to the status of the Cadillac birthplace. He responded on November 15, 1970, that the owner of the house had died, leaving the two parts of the house to the two children. The son Claude Bêche would be willing to sell the left wing which was composed of four rooms and a court, and looked out onto Lamothe Cadillac Street. "See for yourself what you can do in this matter," Boutel wrote, "and let me know."

About this same time Leonard Simons, the president of the Detroit Historical Commission, and his wife Harriet, were planning a trip to southern France. I asked Simons to pay a visit to St. Nicolas in order to see what might be done to help preserve this significant link with Detroit's founder. Simons learned in his meeting with Boutel and the mayor of St. Nicolas that the Cadillac house was indeed available for sale and that the town was anxious to see the house preserved and converted to a community museum. The mayor informed Simons that if the people of Detroit provided a sum of 100,000 French francs (approximately $18,500 at the time), the town of St. Nicolas would add whatever amount was necessary to purchase and restore the house, and to open it to the public as a Cadillac museum.

Upon his return to Detroit, Leonard Simons established a small committee to raise the relatively modest sum necessary in order to realize this long-time objective. Assisting Simons were Glenn Coulter and Walker Cisler who readily accepted the challenge because of their warm personal experiences at St. Nicolas and their great interest in the project. Despite some negative newspaper publicity about Cadillac, ninety-six donors offered the required sum. Contributions of $1,000 were made by General

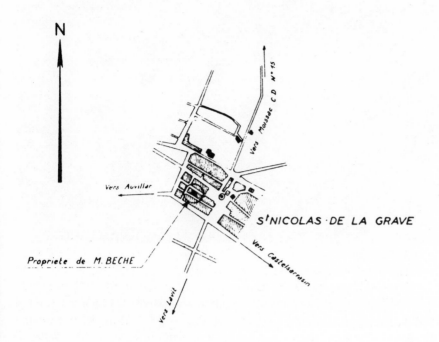

36. Location of Bêche property on Avenue Lamothe Cadillac.

Motors Corporation, Chrysler Corporation, Ford Motor Company, Detroit Edison Company, Mrs. Gerald Slattery, Simons-Michelson Company, William Favorite, and an anonymous organization; the remaining contributions ranged from $25 to $500.

More difficult than the fund raising, however, was obtaining a written agreement from St. Nicolas to confirm the verbal agreement made between Simons and Mayor Lafougere. After much correspondence, the official communication arrived:

> Therefore, after having presented your proposition to my friends of the Municipal Council of St. Nicolas-de-la-Grave, I am first of all asked to thank you for your many efforts to reach a solution for the acquisition and restoration of the house of Lamothe Cadillac.
>
> The Counsel accepts your proposition and the Municipality of St. Nicolas-de-la-Grave will undertake to furnish the additional expenses for the restoration and to set up the interior of the house as its share. Of course, once the work is done, the community of St. Nicolas-de-la-Grave will undertake the maintenance and the conservation of the building.

Obtaining the approval of the Municipal Council and the *Prefet* of Tarn-et-Garonne required much more correspondence and another fourteen months.

The next problem was the question of access to the house. For many years, probably from the very beginning, the Cadillac house had been attached to the two-story building adjoining on the right, and access was gained through a common entrance in that structure. With the two units separated, and since the owner of the adjacent structure did not want to

97

37. Cadillac's birthplace. The court and back of the house with the entrance to the building.

provide a permanent easement for visitors to the Cadillac museum, the only mode of entry would be through the rear, off the court—an unsatisfactory solution. An alternative was to cut a new doorway in the front of the building, but this plan would be counter to our wishes to restore the structure as authentically as possible. This difficulty threatened the continuation of the project.

Finally, after months of one-sided correspondence and lengthy negotiations, it was pointed out that the building originally had a doorway in the front which had been converted into a window. Careful examination of early photographs of the house revealed the unmistakable evidence of this fact. With this roadblock removed there remained only the formal resolution from the Municipal Council of St. Nicolas accepting the gift from Detroit in accordance with the terms originally discussed by Leonard Simons and Mayor Lafougere. I must acknowledge a few of the many people who assisted in concluding the matter: Philippe Wolff, retired head of the History Department of the University of Toulouse, France; John Dunn of Paris, Jacques Dircks-Dilly, the French Consul in Detroit; Claude Charbonniaud, the *Prefet* of Tarn-et-Garonne; Émile Boutel, of St. Nicolas; John Creecy.

The following extract from the record of the resolutions of the Municipal Council of St. Nicolas for the meeting held on August 19, 1972, provides the final approval.

The Mayor read to the Municipal Council the letter of Mr. Leonard Simons, member of the Detroit Historical Commission, expressing the wish to see the birthplace of Lamothe Cadillac, founder of Detroit, acquired by the town of St. Nicolas-de-la-Grave.

To accomplish this, this Society offers the town of St. Nicolas-de-la-Grave a gift of $20,000 U. S., with the condition that the building be acquired, be restored into a museum open to the public, and be properly maintained.

The Detroit Historical Society wishes to specify that this is a question

38. Ceremony in the Mayor's office, St. Nicolas-de-la-Grave, October, 1972. Solan Weeks, Director of the Detroit Historical Museum, presents to Mayor Jean la Fougere the funds for restoration of Cadillac's birthplace. To the left of Weeks stand John Dunn and Mark C. Stevens, past-president of the Detroit Historical Society.

of a single and final gift and that in no way will they consider a further financial obligation.

After listening to this report and following discussion, the Municipal Council agreed:

> to accept the gift and to proceed to acquire the birthplace of Lamothe Cadillac, to make whatever repairs and improvements are necessary, and to make it into a museum and to maintain it in a proper manner.
>
> They further noted that the Detroit Historical Society has consented only to a single and final gift and that further financial assistance will not be sought.

While these negotiations were proceeding, Norman Miller, a representative of Mayor Gribbs's office in Detroit, who was planning a trip to France, agreed to stop in St. Nicolas in order to determine the town's ability to support this museum if it did become a reality. Miller returned with good news: the town of St. Nicolas was involved with the French national government in a major flood control project along the Tarn and Garonne rivers, and because considerable town lands were involved, a substantial government subsidy would be coming into the town annually. From these funds the town government proposed to operate the new museum. The path was now clear to present Detroit's gift to the community of St. Nicolas.

Mark C. Stevens, former president of the Detroit Historical Society, and I planned to make the trip to St. Nicolas, assisted by John Dunne, a former employee of the Detroit Bank and Trust Company who was then living in Paris. On our way to St. Nicolas, our minds were filled with many questions and concerns: who would be responsible for the restoration work; how would we be assured that the work would be done accurately and authentically; who would supervise the project; what guarantee did we have that the project would actually be accomplished once the money had been transferred? On our arrival in St. Nicolas on October 9 our minds were immediately set to rest.

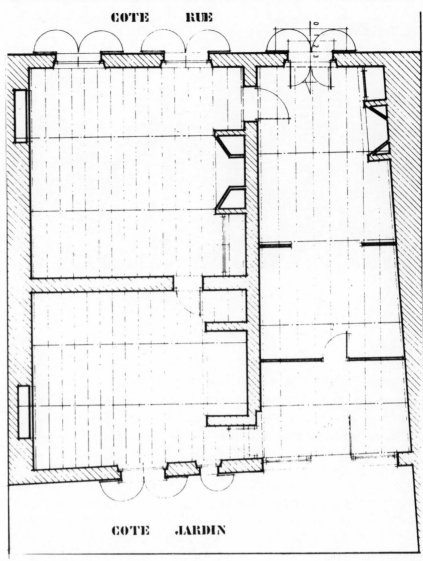

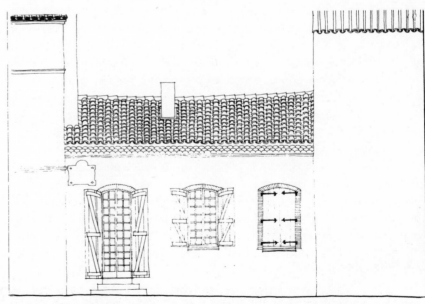

39. Architect's renderings for the restored "Cadillac Museum":

A. Floor plan (top left).

B. New facade with doorway restored (bottom left).

C. Garden side of house (top right).

D. Interior section with two restored fireplaces (bottom right).

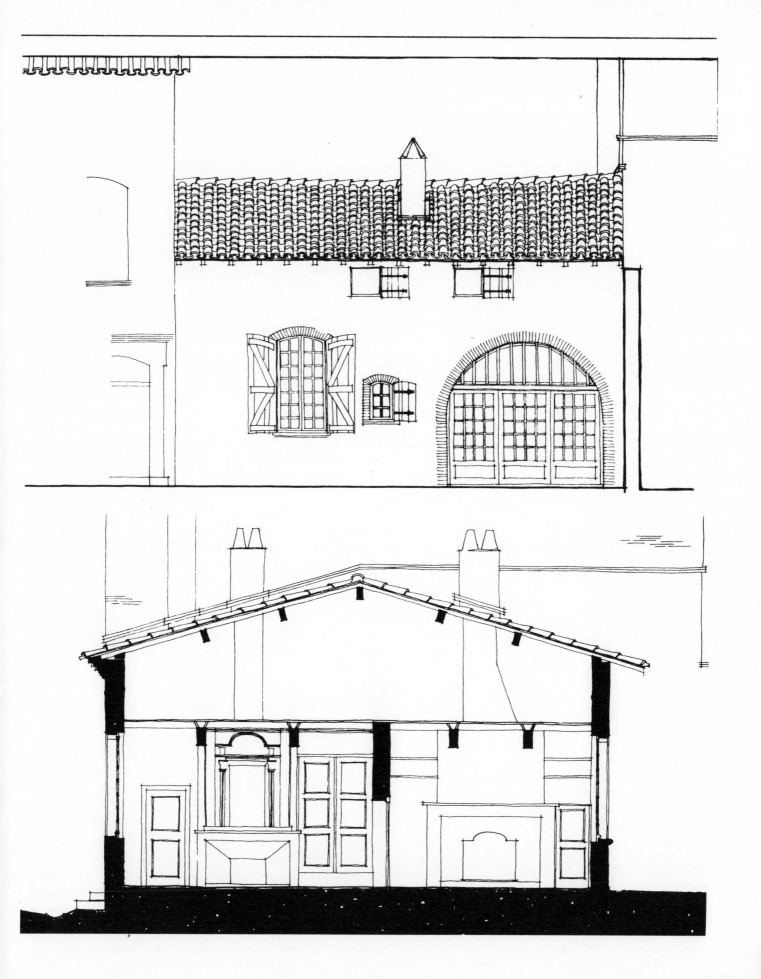

We were met by two representatives of the French Department of Historic Monuments, a father and son team of architects. Roger Salvagnac, the architect in charge of the project, presented us with a detailed set of drawings and specifications which clearly illustrated the present condition of the structure and its projected appearance after restoration. All anticipated expenditures were carefully detailed. We felt no further concern with these two competent historical architects planning and supervising the project.

The formal presentation ceremony was held in the town hall, the eleventh-century structure associated with Richard the Lion-Hearted. Among the dignitaries present were the mayor, Jean Lafougere, the *Prefet* of the District, Claude Charbonniaud, and W. Dixon Boggs, the United States Consul General at Bordeaux. After the brief ceremony was filmed for French national television, we joined in a champagne toast to the bonds of friendship that exist between St. Nicolas and Detroit, listened to the French and American national anthems, and then adjourned to visit the Cadillac house.

The architect Salvagnac pointed out the window that had once been a door. I recalled that when the marker was placed on the house in 1904, reference had been made to the house as having been "reconstructed." The photo of 1904 shows the three windows across the front of the house, and perhaps that was one of the factors considered when this reference was made. On entering the house through the rear, we found that the building had been cleared of debris, but it had received little attention for many years. A hole in the roof where the kitchen chimney once stood had caused extensive dry rot in one of the major beams. Several of the ceiling beams in the parlor were in similar condition as a result of roof leaks. The walls had not been painted for years; the plaster was chipped and peeling. Woodwork, built-in cabinets, cupboards, and doors appeared to be in a good state of preservation. Some of the interior decor that dated from the 18th century was to be kept rather than replaced by replicas from early periods. In all, the weathered and deteriorated brick, the sagging tile roof, the discolored windows, the hand-wrought hinges and hardware, and the huge kitchen fireplace gave the impression of antiquity. Dinners and formal receptions followed by a few days in Paris ended our journey.

Early in the Cadillac house project, at the request of the Detroit Historical Society, Professor Philippe Wolff had recommended René Toujas to fill in the gaps in our knowledge of Cadillac from the original archival and other source material. Toujas compiled the detailed genealogical report, included here, but discovered little new information on Cadillac himself. In the course of his research, Toujas had informed Leonard Simons that although there was no direct proof that the "Cadillac house" was the correct building, the assumption was reasonable. His doubts grew, however, as his letter of January 2, 1972 indicated:

Lamothe Cadillac's birthplace, if it is indeed there where the commemorative plaque is located, and which I am seeking to prove, would be larger than Bêche's lot #1. I found in the archives that Cadillac's father lived in his father-in-law's house (Antoine Péchagut). As both belonged to the "gentry" their house should be larger than that which is offered for sale by Bêche.

RÉPUBLIQUE FRANÇAISE

PREFECTURE DE TARN-ET-GARONNE

Direction des Affaires Financières,
Communales et Départementales

Montauban, le **14 Septembre 1973.**

3e Bureau

Tél. 63-19-41

Référence à rappeler :

N° GG/GG   26 sept. 1973   *Le Préfet de Tarn-et-Garonne*

                                  à **M**onsieur le MAIRE

                                  de SAINT-NICOLAS-DE-LA-GRAVE

                                  S/C de M. le Sous-Préfet de Castelsarrasin

X   OBJET : Inscription sur l'inventaire supplémentaire des
            Monuments Historiques.

    P. J. : I.

           J'ai l'honneur de vous adresser, sous ce pli, copie
    de l'arrêté de M. le Ministre des Affaires Culturelles en
    date du I8 Juillet I973 portant inscription sur l'inventaire
    supplémentaire des Monuments Historiques des façades et des
    toitures de la maison où naquit le Chevalier de Lamothe-
    Cadillac.

                                          LE PREFET,

COPIE transmise à :

- Monsieur l'ARCHITECTE DES BATIMENTS
  DE FRANCE
            MONTAUBAN

40. On September 14, 1973, the prefecture of Tarn-et-Garonne informed the mayor of St. Nicolas-de-la-Grave that the Ministry of Cultural Affairs of France had decreed on July 18, 1973, "the facades and roofs of the house located in St. Nicolas-de-la-Grave, where Lamothe Cadillac was born" an historic monument.

Since my last letter, I found in the Montauban archives that Antoine Péchagut, grandfather of Lamothe Cadillac, lived on the Avenue Faure, where the Bêche house with the commemorative plaque is located. I now have to find the exact spot on the street where Antoine Péchagut's house stood. I'll keep you informed, but it is valuable to know, for now, that the Cadillac birthplace is indeed on the street where tradition has located it.

Toujas came to the opinion that the Cadillac house had disappeared, although "it was in the Avenue Faure, near the public square, almost at the location where tradition places it; the present structure dates from the 19th century." We were concerned over this new information and curious to know the facts upon which he based his opinions. I asked William Bostick, administrator of the Detroit Institute of Arts, who was planning a trip to France, to visit St. Nicolas and to check on the progress of the restoration and also to visit Toujas and discuss with him his reasons for believing that the house currently on the site was of the 19th century. Bostick wrote me on July 1, 1973 that,

> after a long discussion about the house, Mr. Toujas showed and explained to me how residences of this type were built in the 17th and 18th centuries. They were built of bricks made of earth and straw dried in the sun. In France it is called "maison construites en torchis"

[mud-built house]. Only very important buildings, such as the church in St. Nicolas, would have been built of kiln fired brick.

Toujas agreed that the present house stood on the site of Cadillac's birthplace, and, Bostick wrote, considerable progress was being made in the renovation of the house. Toujas's personal opinion about the authenticity of the house concerned us, but we felt that the documentation of the authenticity of the construction materials should be verified by the architects from the French National Landmarks Department who were supervising the restoration.

This question was uppermost in my mind when I returned to France in 1974 for the dedication of the newly restored Cadillac home. For this occasion the Detroit Historical Society had organized a special ten-day tour of southern France. Twenty-one members of the Detroit Historical Society, led by Mark C. Stevens, and whose names I record here, made the pilgrimage.

Mrs. Henry D. Brown
Mr. Glenn M. Coulter
Mrs. Leland W. Foster
Mrs. Elizabeth Grant
Mrs. Wendell C. Goddard
Mrs. Adelaide Hajduk
Miss Gail Hajduk
Miss Beatrice Jobagy
Mr. and Mrs. Lloyd Kissick

Mr. and Mrs. H. J. Knighton
Mr. and Mrs. Frank J. McGinnis
Dr. and Mrs. Don W. McLean
Dr. Raymond C. Miller
Mr. and Mrs. Stanley Seitz
Mr. Mark C. Stevens
Mr. Solan W. Weeks
(Leonard Simons joined us in France)

The trip began on May 3, 1974. At Bordeaux the group was treated to a tour of the beautifully restored city followed by a reception in the home of Mr. and Mrs. W. Dixon Boggs, the United States Consul General in Bordeaux. The next several days of touring historic sites was capped with a visit to the town of Cadillac on the Garonne River, where the ancient Chateau Cadillac had stood. Lamothe Cadillac must have passed this way many times on his trips to the major port of Bordeaux, and it has been speculated that he may have assumed the name of this chateau as his own.

On the afternoon of May 8 we arrived at the modern hotel, Moulin de Moissac, which served as our headquarters during our visit to "Cadillac Country." The following morning we were met by Mayor Lafougere and Leonce Meyson, the assistant governor for the district. After a bus tour of points of interest, the Detroit delegation gave a dinner for the French dignitaries and presented them with a number of gifts for the new museum. Included were a proclamation from Mayor Coleman Young, a color photograph of the Detroit skyline, a photograph of the bust of Cadillac that had been given to Detroit by the French Government, several Detroit-American flags, a number of volumes on the history of Detroit, and copies of Cadillac-related manuscripts. The next day we visited the Romanesque church and cloisters of the Moissac abbey and the local museum, followed by a visit to the governor's residence at Castelsarrasin and luncheon as the guests of M. and Mme. Meyson.

The old Carmelite church, now a civic center, where Cadillac was buried, and a visit to the house in Castelsarrasin where Cadillac had lived his last years were next on our schedule. Champagne, with appropriate

toasts and rhetoric occupied us until 4:15 P.M. But the dedication of the museum in St. Nicolas was to have begun at 4:00! The flashing blue lights of a police escort led us through a gentle mist to Cadillac's birthplace.

As we approached the town, lines of people crowded along the route; the little street where the Cadillac house stood was swarming with people, including the entire student body of the local school. While everyone waited patiently, we carried the assortment of gifts that we had brought into the house, ducking under the tricolor ribbon that stretched across the front door, and then presented ourselves for the dedication and opening of the Cadillac Museum.

Mark Stevens acted as official spokesman. His diary describes the scene.

There I was, framed in the doorway, looking out over a sea of heads including a large delegation of the very young. I didn't much like my job. "Mesdames distinguées, et Messieurs également distingués," I began, and perhaps anachronistically presented to their friends and close neighbors our collaborators in this enterprise: M. Meyson, M. Lafougere, and M. Salvagnac (M. Charbonniaud was not able to attend). Somehow, I felt less lonely now, and my new neighbors were beaming appreciatively. I was still aware, however, of the presence of Television Français, and of Frank McGinnis who had a tape recorder going and was snapping pictures like crazy. My comments were necessarily banal. Every time I got stuck for a word, I would confer, *sotto voce,* with M. Meyson, who would supply it, and this collaboration pleased the natives immeasurably.

41. American delegation and French dignitaries walk past the market square of St. Nicolas-de-la-Grave on their way to dedicate the Cadillac Museum.

105

They were exceedingly tolerant of my foibles of grammar, conjugation, gender, and what not. Dixon Boggs was beaming encouragement. I made the several presentations to Mayor Lafougere. When it came to the proclamation by Mayor Coleman Young in English with French translation, I said that because of the weather, I wouldn't bother them with the whole text. There was a general negative reaction. It would be meaningless for me to read the English, so I waded into the French. I drizzled on, along with the rain, and all things have an end.

After the presentation of gifts, Mayor Lafougere delivered an impressive address that closed with the formal, "Long live the United States! Long live France!" Leonard N. Simons, acting in his official capacity as President of the Detroit Historical Commission, then cut the ribbon and the Cadillac Museum was officially opened to visitors. Mr. Salvagnac, the architect in charge of the restoration, had done a splendid job. Gone were the mushrooms which had been growing from the ceiling, gone was the peeled plaster, and gone were the rotted wood beams which I had seen on my previous visit.

The four-room house with high (twelve or thirteen foot) beamed ceilings throughout was tastefully restored. The walls were unpainted white cement, and the closely spaced ceiling beams and other trim were painted light turquoise, a popular color in the area and historically correct for the house. The floor was made of red-orange tile also typical of the region. The room that now served as the entrance and the room directly behind it that led to the courtyard were outfitted with display cases which held important Cadillac-related documents on loan from various archival depositories. The 18th-century fireplace and large wooden cupboard had been returned and restored.

The main living room to the right of the entry room was sparsely furnished with antiques on loan from the museum in Moissac. The curator, Mlle. Vidal, had selected them to reflect the period in which Cadillac was born and lived. Among the exhibitions was a huge, hand-carved, four-poster bed, a wooden chest, and a large armoire of the type that might have graced the house in 1658. The spacious kitchen, located directly behind, had a huge fireplace with a wooden mantle that appeared to be at least six feet high and eight feet across. A large wooden sideboard cupboard stocked with period china, glassware, and silverware, and a large chest, table, several chairs, and a unique yarn reel completed the decoration.

The focal point of the courtyard at the rear of the house was a large rectangular flower garden with a border of red flowers and a center of white flowers planted to spell out St. Nicolas and Detroit.

Following the ceremony I told the architect Salvagnac of the questions which had been raised concerning the authenticity of the house, and I asked if he would verity the authenticity of the building materials. We were standing in the street in front of the building. He pointed out where the bricks which were used in the Cadillac house tied in with the bricks in the structure adjacent to it. He said the two structures had been built at the

42. Autographs: the Detroit and the French delegations "sign in" on May 10, 1974.

same time and that the doorway of the house reflected the carpentry of the 17th and 18th centuries. In his opinion the Cadillac house was originally accessible to the street through that door which gave access to both sides of the building. I asked if the Cadillac house had ever been a two-story structure since the bricks on the adjacent structure above the roof line of the Cadillac house protruded as if a building had been removed. He assured me that the house had never been any taller than at present, and that it was very typical for houses of that period and locality to be constructed in such a fashion to facilitate future expansion. I commented about Toujas's concern over the age and type of brick, and that Toujas did not believe that fired bricks were used in ordinary homes of the Cadillac period. Mayor Lafougere said that his house, built in the 1600s, located on the market square around the corner from the Cadillac house, was built of the same type of brick. Meyson also assured me that many other early houses in that part of France were constructed of the identical fired brick.

Salvagnac said that in restoring the Cadillac house they had taken great pains to replace the bricks, which he called *foraines,* with old bricks of the same type salvaged from structures of the same period, and this procedure was followed with all of the replacement parts which were utilized during the course of the restoration. Salvagnac presented me with a certificate from the French National Department of Historic Monuments which indicated that the facade and roof of the Cadillac birthplace had been added to the supplemental list of the National Register of Historic Landmarks on July 18, 1973, further to confirm and verity the authenticity of the structure. Thus, with the archivist documenting the site and the architect verifying the antiquity of the structure on the site, I felt confident that at last this question had been satisfactorily resolved.

At the conclusion of the tour of the house we adjourned to the Council Chambers of the town hall for a champagne reception, a *vin d'honneur,* commemorating the bonds that exist between the two nations and two communities. In the evening we were hosted by the mayor and town council at a festive banquet in the barrel-vaulted chamber of the 11th-century Chateau Terrides. In a brief after-dinner speech that Leonard Simons had prepared in French for the occasion, he remarked that after such a large meal with so many delicious courses he "regretted that he had only one stomach to give for his country."

The festivities ended, and we concluded our visit to the "Cadillac Country" with a feeling of warm friendship toward the citizens of St. Nicolas. We were proud of the role we had played in this people-to-people project which united our two communities through the preservation of this tangible link with the heritage we jointly and proudly share.

Leonard N. Simons, president, and only remaining member of the first Detroit Historical Commission, has served continuously on that body since 1946, under seven mayors.

Cadillac: A Retrospective View
Leonard N. Simons

During my thirty years of tenure as a Detroit Historical Commissioner, I assumed the responsibility for reading all available literature on the life of Cadillac. The more I read, the more fascinated I became because of the conflicting stories of this man's life. I visited the "Cadillac country" in France twice, and I met and corresponded with those who shared my interest, as a non-professional historian, in France and America. With the help of my friend Philippe Wolff, retired professor and chairman of history at Toulouse University, and supported by the Detroit Historical Society, René Toujas, archivist of the Department of Haute-Garonne (France), was asked to undertake research on Cadillac and his family, to verify the accuracy of previous reporting, and to locate new documentary evidence. Through the good offices of Mathieu Méras, Directeur des Services of Tarn-et-Garonne (France), and president of its archaeological society, I met Henri Négrié, a physician in the service of the French Navy who had spent the last ten years of his life studying and writing on Cadillac. Part of his findings are incorporated in this volume. (I must report, sadly, that Dr. Négrié died last year at the age of eighty-five.) Hence, my involvement in the career of Cadillac is long standing. Here, I offer my personal, but I trust objective, view of the founder of Detroit.

After careful readings of the life and career of Cadillac by past historians of the City of Detroit—Levi Bishop, Silas Farmer, Clarence Burton, Milo Quaife, and George Stark—and other commentators, such as the Jesuit priests Jean Delanglez and George Paré, it was inevitable that I, too, should reconstruct a picture of Cadillac the man. I am convinced that Cadillac was not as great a man as many historians have described him, nor as evil as other historians have claimed. The truth lies somewhere in between. On balance, I view him as the type of 18th-century military man that one would expect to find as a servant of his government, a soldier sent to open unexplored lands in a new world, to find ways to control the Indians there, to fight the enemies, particularly the British, of his country, and, quite naturally, to create a reputation and fortune for himself.

What was Cadillac really like? We may never have the definitive answer. After having read the many accounts and documents available, I try in this retrospective view to picture the man.

I visualize Cadillac as a pioneer adventurer with the courage, fortitude, and stamina to tackle any assignment. In his efforts to accomplish that which he had set his heart and mind on doing in North America, for France as well as for himself, he would tolerate no interference from any group or individual. In his fight for survival among the natives, as well as in his dealing with his contemporaries, who, like Cadillac, were also opportunists, he lived by his wits and by his audacity. He played for the greatest of stakes—his own survival.

One can understand why a man in his situation may have considered necessary the taking of liberties with truth, and the exploiting of some people in order to reach his goals. Those were hectic days in the New

109

World. He was striving to plant a new civilization in an ancient wilderness. Certainly he made many enemies, chiefly because he would not let others force their will on him, or because he had deprived others of making money at posts he commanded. Some were jealous of his authority and his contacts with the top echelon of government in Old and New France. Ambiguous, often slanderous or libelous comments were written about him by those who disliked him for a variety of reasons. Yet even those contemporaries who criticized his actions found him keen and cautious, resolute in holding his ground. He would neither yield right of judgment nor his prerogatives as commandant. His position of leadership made him vulnerable to accusations of wrongdoing, but his loyalty to King and country was never in dispute. He was strong-willed, and perhaps without such men in the New World at the beginning of the 18th century, there may not have been a United States of America today.

The official correspondence of the government of New France in Canada records valuable information about Cadillac that shows him to have been of great assistance to Governor Frontenac. A solid friendship was created between these two men. Count Pontchartrain (Louis Phélypeaux), Secretary of State of the Department of Marine in Paris, was another valuable friend of Cadillac. Such friendships indicate the confidence the top-level men of France had in Cadillac, and are a measure of his ability and the respect it commanded. A man in Cadillac's position usually makes friends and enemies, and Cadillac had no interest in attaining popularity at the price of his goals. Although he had duties to perform that unquestionably would irritate many, he accomplished that which his superiors expected of him.

When Frontenac appointed Cadillac commandant of Michilimackinac, confident of the latter's ability to cope with Indian opposition, he wrote to Count Pontchartrain that Cadillac was

> a man of rank, full of capability and valor . . . . we could not make a better choice than to appoint Lieutenant de Lamothe Cadillac, captain of the troops of the detachment of the Marine, whose valor, wisdom, experience, and good conduct have been manifested on several occasions.

When Frontenac died in November 1698, Cadillac's proposed arrangements to establish a post on the Detroit River were interrupted. Undaunted by Frontenac's successor, who did not approve of the idea, Cadillac went to Paris for an interview with Count Pontchartrain and a personal examination by King Louis XIV of his project to establish a colony at Detroit. He was successful: "The King granted every request and returned Cadillac to New France with a commission signed by Count Pontchartrain to establish a trading post wherever he desired."

Thus, Detroit came into existence. Cadillac picked the spot on which to build a village called "Fort Pontchartrain du troit" in honor of his friend and benefactor, Jérôme (son of Louis) Phélypeaux, Count de Pontchartrain, who was the Colonial Minister of Marine when Cadillac sought permission to establish the colony. The Count, head of colonial affairs for fifteen years, was bitterly criticized, as was Cadillac, by his enemies. In Cadillac's day, both Old and New France were governed by cabal and intrigue. Officials, priests, and traders competed with each other in devising schemes for personal and churchly aggrandizement. Hundreds of old letters show how these various groups were divided by jealousy and distrust.

In Detroit, Cadillac was lord of all the property, millions of unclaimed and uncultivated acres. Even the church building with its vestments and paraphernalia, by a decision of the King, belonged to Cadillac. The first settlers in Detroit obviously were not a simple, contented, Arcadian folk. The wilderness village was a place of tension, nervousness, and unrest. The Jesuit Order was the dominant power in the New World. Cadillac inherited the power conflict between the Order and Governor Frontenac. Contemporary correspondence clearly shows how the Order hindered Cadillac's projects and how he in turn opposed their plans.

Thus, it is understandable that the Jesuit priests wrote disparagingly about Cadillac, with whom they were continually quarreling. He would not take their orders; it was that simple. "In matters pertaining to the civil state, the responsibility is mine, and I will decide what I think is in the King's best interest," Cadillac announced. Under these circumstances, Jesuit historians could not be expected to compliment Cadillac. The Jesuits were not wrong in their attitudes and viewpoints, nor was Cadillac in his. It appears that the best judges, those in the position to evaluate Cadillac's actions, were the King of France and his deputies, the colonial minister and the governor-general of New France. History records that these men agreed that Cadillac was serving France properly and that he should continue to be the head of the village he founded.

The love and affection of a wife and children are some indication of a man's worth. Cadillac's marriage was happy. His wife followed her husband from Montreal to Detroit, traveling 1,000 miles in open canoes, over all kinds of terrain and in all weather, to reach Detroit, traveling with the tough *coureurs de bois* and Indians. Cadillac must have had many redeeming qualities to deserve this tribute. His wife was his companion during those long and difficult years in the wilderness, and she bore him thirteen children.

We have the story that when Madame Cadillac was preparing to leave Quebec to join her husband at Detroit in 1701, several ladies said to her, "It might do if you were going to a pleasant country where you could have good company, but it is impossible to conceive how you can be willing to go to a desert country where there is nothing to do but die of ennui." She is said to have replied, "A woman who loves her husband as she should, has no stronger attraction than his company, wherever he may be; everything else should be indifferent to her."

The accumulated reports show Cadillac as a courageous, young soldier who sought adventure and money in the wilderness of the New World. Courage was required; what he accomplished was not the reward of a coward.

Much comment has been stimulated by the fact that Antoine Laumet took the name of Lamothe Cadillac when he came to Canada. Accusations have never been specific. I am not convinced that there is any truth to the intimations that he had to leave St. Nicolas-de-la-Grave for some undisclosed reason. Of what was Cadillac guilty in taking a new name at the age of twenty-five? Countless Europeans did that in those days. (My own relatives adopted new names when they came from Europe many years ago, certainly not to conceal some "dark deed" in the past.) It was not unusual for French families in the late seventeenth and early eighteenth centuries to have several sons with as many different surnames. Each chose the name he wanted, for whatever reason. Cadillac's oldest brother changed his name to François Laumet *Lacousille*. The practice is common today in America, and, of course, quite legal. Clearly a name change does not infer wrongdoing, although the possibility remains. In the case of Cadillac, without a shred of supporting evidence, the accusation must be dismissed as simple malice.

Finally, in an evaluation of Cadillac the man, we must remember that our historical record does not begin until he is nineteen years old, still unmarried, living in a tiny farm community, with no promise of a future. In this there is reason enough for Cadillac and his two brothers to have joined the French army. Cadillac soon left France for adventure in the unknown, the largely unexplored New France. Young people dream of thrilling lives, as Cadillac must have; but Cadillac made his dreams come true in spite of all opposition. No matter his motives, he made a significant and permanent contribution to history, establishing the first important outpost of European civilization west of the Alleghenies, the oldest city in the Middle West. Above the flood of controversy, one fact remains secure: Cadillac founded the city of Detroit, and for that he deserves our respect and the honor we accord his memory on this our 275th anniversary.

Appendices

Glossary

Arpent
An old agrarian measure; a square arpent was approximately .85 of an acre.

Company of the Colony of Canada
A stock company formed in 1700 by some leading merchants of Canada; dealt mainly in animal pelts: beaver, elk, bear, deer, raccoon, muskrat.

Coureur de bois
Unlicensed French who traded with the Indians and sold to both the French and the English.

Intendant
The highest civil officer of a colony; his actions carried the authority of royal sanction.

League
Measure of length that varied, but usually 2.4-2.6 miles.

Livre
Old unit of currency, based on silver weight, equal to something under twenty cents.

Pound
English equivalent of French word *livre,* above.

Recollects
Catholic order (also called Observants) of the Franciscans.

Sieur
Old form of address, for *monsieur,* from *seigneur* (sire).

Voyageurs
French-Canadian canoemen, usually from the St. Lawrence valley, who worked for the beaver traders.

Abbreviations

Burton, *Detroit*	Burton, Clarence M. *Early Detroit*. Detroit, n.d.
Burton, *Cadillac*	———. *Cadillac's Village, or Detroit Under Cadillac*. Detroit, 1896.
Burton, *Building*	———. *The Building of Detroit*. Detroit, 1912.
Burton, *MPHS*	———. "A Visit to the Home of Cadillac," *Michigan Pioneer and Historical Society*, 38 (1912).
DCB	*Dictionary of Canadian Biography*.
Delanglez, "Early Years"	Delanglez, Jean. "Cadillac's Early Years in America," *Mid-America*, 15 (1944).
Delanglez, "Genesis"	———. "The Genesis and Building of Detroit," *Mid-America*, 19 (1948).
Delanglez, "Cadillac"	———. "Cadillac at Detroit, *Mid-America*, 19 (1948).
Delanglez, "Last Years"	———. "Cadillac's Last Years," *Mid-America*, 22 (1951).
Farmer, *History*	Farmer, Silas. *The History of Detroit and Michigan*.² Detroit, 1889.
Lewis, *Detroit*	Lewis, Ferris E. Detroit, *A Wilderness Outpost of Old France*. Detroit, 1951.
Margry, *MetD*	Margry, Pierre. *Mémoires et Documents*, vol. 5. Paris, 1887.
Méras, *Tarn*	Méras, Mathieu. *Tarn-et-Garonne*. Montauban, n. d.
Négrié, "Pioneer"	Négrié, Henri. "A Pioneer of New France, Lamothe-Cadillac," *Bulletin, Archaeological Society, Tarn-et-Garonne*, 99 (1974).
Paré, *Church*	Paré, George. *The Catholic Church in Detroit, 1701–1888*. Detroit, 1951.
Simons, "Cadillac"	Simons, Leonard N. "Cadillac Did It."
Stark, *City*	Stark, George W. *City of Destiny, The Story of Detroit*. Detroit, 1943.
Toujas, *Destin*	Toujas, René. *Le Destin extraordinaire du gascon Lamothe-Cadillac, fondateur de Detroit*. Montauban, 1974.

115

Sources

The essays and commentaries derive mainly from archival materials in Europe, Canada, and America. The major archival sources are:

Paris
  Archives of the Colonies
  Archives of the Marine
  Bastille, Arsenal Library
  Gironde Archives
  Ministry of Foreign Affairs
  National Library

Haute-Garonne Archives
Tarn-et-Garonne Archives
Toulouse Municipal Archives
St. Nicolas-de-la-Grave Municipal Archives
Rome, Archives of the Society of Jesus

Quebec
  Archives of the Province of Quebec
  Archives of the Seminary of Quebec,
   Laval University

Chicago, E. E. Ayer Collection of the Newberry Library

Detroit
  Burton Collection of the Detroit Public Library
  Detroit Historical Museum

The editor of *Mid-America,* the journal that carried the articles on Cadillac which Father Delanglez had intended to incorporate into a single volume on Cadillac and the Jesuits, compiled a bibliography of Delanglez's sources (Delanglez, "Last Years"). To this listing may now be added that for the Cadillac citation in the *Dictionary of Canadian Biography.*

The Contributors

Henry D. Brown, past director, Detroit Historical Museum.

Philip P. Mason, director, University Archives, Wayne State University.

Henri Négrié, past president, Archaeological Society of Tarn-et-Garonne (France).

Frank R. Place, Department of History, Wayne State University.

Leonard N. Simons, president, Detroit Historical Commission.

René Toujas, archivist, Department Haute-Garonne (France).

Solan Weeks, director, Detroit Historical Museum.

The manuscript was prepared for publication by Alice Nigoghosian. The book was designed by Richard Kinney, assisted by Mary Primeau. Cover illustration by Julie Paul. The typeface for the text and display is Optima designed by Hermann Zapf about 1958.

The text is printed on Glatfelter's Springforge paper. The book is bound in Carolina cover CIS. Manufactured in the United States of America.